INCENTIVES IN GOVERNMENT CONTRACTING

R. Preston McAfee and John McMillan

Incentives in Government Contracting

UNIVERSITY OF TORONTO PRESS
Toronto Buffalo London

© University of Toronto Press 1988
Toronto Buffalo London
Printed in Canada
Reprinted in 2018
ISBN 0-8020-6638-0
ISBN 978-1-4875-8140-4 (paper)

Canadian Cataloguing in Publication Data

McAfee, R.Preston
 Incentives in government contracting

 Includes bibliographical references and index.
 ISBN 0-8020-6638-0

 1. Public contracts. 2. Public contracts - Ontario.
 3. Government purchasing. I. McMillan, John, 1951-
 II. Title.

 JF1525.P85M22 1988   350.71'1   C87-093728-6

Contents

Figures

Tables

Acknowledgments

We owe thanks for their comments to David Conklin and Jack Levenstein of the Ontario Economic Council; Richard Harris and James MacKinnon of Queen's University; Robert Bish of the University of Victoria; Åke Blomqvist, James Davies, Peter Howitt, and John Whalley of the University of Western Ontario; and two anonymous referees. We also owe thanks to participants in seminars in which the work was presented: the Conference on Strategic Behaviour and the Theory of the Firm at the University of Western Ontario; the Econometric Society Meetings in Dallas; and seminars at the Ontario Economic Council, the California Institute of Technology, the University of Arizona, the University of British Columbia, the University of California, San Diego, the University of California, Los Angeles, the University of Toronto, Tsukuba University, and the University of Western Ontario.

R. Armstrong of the Ministry of Natural Resources, V. Gibbons of the Management Board of Cabinet, J. Kryzanowski of Ontario Hydro, T. Spearin of the Ministry of Industry and Trade, D.E. Thrasher of the Ministry of Transportation and Communications, A.W. Thurston of the Ministry of Government Services, and J. Wickens of the Ministry of Industry and Trade generously provided information on Ontario government contracting practices and helped prevent the project from being a purely academic exercise.

Veena Mishra and Richard Jones provided able research assistance, and Yvonne Adams, Brenda Campbell, Leslie Farrant, and Marg Gower expertly typed several drafts of the manuscript.

INCENTIVES IN GOVERNMENT CONTRACTING

1

Government Contracting

1. THE SCOPE OF THIS STUDY

Many observers express concern about the ever-increasing size of government budget deficits. Those who seek solutions to the deficit problem usually look either for government services that can be cut in order to reduce government spending or for ways of raising more revenue in taxes. Both approaches are controversial, because either approach would harm certain groups within society.

Obviously, a painless way of reducing deficits would be to supply the same government services at a lower cost. Any policy that achieved this result would seem to involve getting something for nothing; nevertheless, this study will argue that, by changing the way in which the government pays the firms from which it buys goods and services, the same government programs can indeed be had at a lower cost.

The national, regional, and local governments in a typical modern market economy together spend between one-quarter and one-third of national income on goods and services (this figure excludes transfer payments). Of this amount, perhaps one-half, or up to one-sixth of national income as a whole, is paid by governments to firms. Thus the potential benefits from a study of government contracting procedures are significant. If some way can be found to improve contracting procedures, even to only a small extent, the government's dollar savings could be large. (Though these savings would not, of course, be large enough in themselves to eliminate the budget deficit.)

Government agencies contract out a wide range of work to private firms: building bridges and roads; constructing nuclear power stations; snow clearing; maintaining public buildings; building low-income public housing; providing technical consulting services; conducting opinion polls and advertising campaigns. This study will investigate the possibility of reducing the government's costs by changing the design of the contracts under which such tasks are carried out.

The most common type of government-firm contract is the fixed-price contract, under which the price is arranged before the work is begun. This study will recommend ways in which a government can lower its payments while using fixed-price contracts. The other form of contract in common use is the cost-plus contract, under which the government pays the contractor a fee plus his costs in carrying out the project. The present study will discuss the drawbacks of using cost-plus contracts and show that it is always possible to devise an alternative contract that is less costly to the government than a cost-plus contract. The study will give special attention to the advantages of one type of alternative contract, the incentive contract. The incentive contract makes payment depend upon the contractor's performance; it is analogous to private-sector payment schemes such as royalties and commissions.

The government's payment is the sum of the production cost incurred by the contractor and the contractor's profit: any reduction in the government's payment must therefore involve reducing either production cost or profit, or both. This study will suggest several ways of improving government contracting procedures. These remedies involve both inducing contractors to reduce the costs they incur in doing government work and lowering the profits contractors earn from such work.

Many firms might actually prefer lower profits than they currently earn under government contracts. Under a fixed-price contract, the government pays the firm a definite sum of money for doing the work, regardless of the costs the firm actually incurs. The costs of carrying out any project are never perfectly predictable. The fixed-price contract requires the firm to bear all of the risk of unpredictable cost increases. To the extent that the firm prefers to avoid risk, the government must offer the firm a relatively high profit in order to make the risk acceptable to the firm. Under an incentive contract, however, the government bears some of this risk. In exchange for the government's sheltering it from risk, the firm might be willing to accept a lower profit rate. Thus, as we shall argue in what follows, both the firm and the government would be better off: the firm because it faced less risk, and the government because its costs would be lower.

The government could also lower contractors' profits (though not, this time, with the firms' acquiescence) by increasing the competition among firms for its contracts. In some instances, we shall argue, the contracts currently in use induce too little competition in bidding for government work. Under some types of contract, moreover, the firm is not given sufficient incentive to hold down the costs it incurs; as a result, cost overruns are common in government projects, especially in projects carried out under cost-plus contracts. A different form of contract would give the firm incentives to seek ways of keeping costs low.

It might be questioned whether this approach to government contracting is fair to the firms involved. The point of view taken in this study is that such a question is irrelevant. In a free society, the government cannot coerce a firm into accepting a contract; the contract must offer the firm a rate of return no smaller than the rate it could earn by working elsewhere. The market puts a lower bound on how much profit a firm can generally earn from a government contract: the contention of this study is that the government should try to ensure that the profits earned by its contractors are as little as possible above this market-determined minimum. Profits are, of course, essential to the functioning of a market economy. But excessive profits—that is, profits greater than the normal rate of return—are not. If firms are earning larger than normal profits from government contracts, then taxpayers' money is being wasted; the government is, in effect, making a gift of taxpayers' dollars to the firms' shareholders and employees.

In addition to undertaking both theoretical and empirical analysis of the optimal design of government contracts, this study will estimate the consequences of increasing competition among firms bidding for contracts; it will analyse the effects of offering preferential treatment to domestic firms in government procurement; it will discuss the possibilities for privatization, asking whether particular public goods and services should be produced in-house by a government agency or whether they should be produced under contract by a private firm; and it will describe and classify actual government contracting procedures, drawing lessons from past experience in government contracting in both Canada and the United States. The reader can obtain a quick overview of the study by going directly to the last chapter.

One question will undoubtedly arise: why have the policies advocated in this book not been put into practice already? If our proposals are really worthwhile, then why have government officials with years of experience and therefore a thorough understanding of contracting problems failed to develop these solutions for themselves? Our response to this question is that the book's analysis makes use of some new results in economic theory. Analysis of the costs and the benefits of different contracting policies inevitably involves some subtle technical problems; the theoretical tools for handling these problems had not been developed until recently.

The suggestions for changes in contracting practices made in this study should not be taken as implicit criticisms of the job that the public servants responsible for contracting have been doing and currently are doing. On the contrary, our remedies would make even more use than is made at present of the knowledge that the individual official has acquired through experience in dealing with a particular industry.

That an independent study of government practices can yield a significant return is illustrated by recent US experience. The President's Private Sector Survey on Cost Control (the Grace Commission) found that the United States Government could save $424 billion over three years by reducing waste, inefficiency, and fraud (United States 1984). However, the Grace Commission's report has been criticized on two grounds. First, the recommendations reflect the biases of the commission's members: several of the money-saving proposals involve eliminating specific programs that, according to the value judgments of the members of the commission, the government should not be undertaking. Second, it is not clear how the commission arrived at its estimates of dollar savings: in some cases, these estimates seem to be little more than guesses. The present study avoids the first criticism by deliberately adopting a narrow scope: we take the range of the government's activities as given, and the question we ask is simply how the existing government programs can be undertaken at lower cost. The study avoids criticisms of the second sort by basing its estimates of amounts to be saved on a rigorously formulated economic model.

The presumption that the government's objective is to minimize its costs of having work done may not always be appropriate. Sometimes governments use their procurement policies to further particular social or political ends: the transfer of technology, for example, or the encouragement of small business, or the direction of work opportunities to regions of high unemployment. Yet even when the government is pursuing some objective other than simple economy, this study is relevant. A rational evaluation of whether social programs are worthwhile can only be made by weighing their costs and benefits. The present study provides half of the basis for this comparison; that is, it provides ways of measuring the extent to which social or political objectives increase the costs of a project above its minimum possible level. In other words, the study shows how to attach a price tag to the social benefits pursued via procurement policies.

2. COMPARISON WITH PRIVATE-SECTOR CONTRACTING

How do public sector contracting practices compare with private sector contracting practices? Firms often subcontract some of their requirements to other firms. Although this study's discussion will be put in terms of the government's use of the services of a firm, the principles that determine the optimal characteristics of a contract are equally applicable to contracts written between firms.

For political reasons, contracting in the public sector must not only be conducted honestly but be seen to be conducted honestly. This requirement of visibility and accountability usually rules out closed negotiations and requires the use of sealed-bid tenders, the opening of the bids in public, and the awarding of the contract to the lowest bidder.

In contrast to the public sector, private industry usually uses competitive bidding only for special purposes. These purposes include buying unique or specialized items and buying in markets in which the buyer has little information about the identity of the alternative suppliers and their prices. The private sector usually uses informal negotiations rather than competitive bidding.

Even when private industry does use competitive bidding, the procedures it follows are often different from the procedures required in the public sector. In the public sector, the contract must by law be awarded to the lowest responsible bidder. In contrast, when bids are solicited in the private sector, the bidding is sometimes merely a way of narrowing the field to a few firms, with which the buyer then conducts private negotiations over price (Westing et al 1976: 198; England 1970: 597).

In the private sector, then, the selection of a contractor and the terms of the contract are usually determined by negotiation, while in the public sector the usual mechanism is competitive bidding. What can negotiations achieve? Negotiations provide flexibility. Arrangements for the sharing of risks can be made. If there is some particular risk that one party is better able to bear than the other party, then the first party might agree to accept responsibility for the risk in exchange for some concession on price. During the negotiations, the buyer can enquire about the potential supplier's costs and ask for justification of the potential supplier's price quotation. The buyer can insist that a potential supplier not take advantage of a privileged position, such as having lower costs than his competitors as a result of being the incumbent supplier. Finally, once a private sector buyer has received bids from some potential suppliers, he can, unlike the government, decide to allow the bidders to revise their bids. If the buyer believes that the bids he has received include unreasonably high profit margins, he may be able, by judiciously releasing information about the bids, to induce the bidders to revise their bids downwards. It might be enough to simply inform bidders whether or not they have submitted the lowest bid (Aljian 1958: 9-34; England 1970: 599-601).

It is sometimes suggested that the inability to use negotiations unduly constrains the public sector purchasing agent relative to his private sector counterpart. The lack of flexibility that results from the inability to negotiate, it is claimed, hinders the government official in his search for the lowest possible price.

However, the results presented in this study suggest that the difference between what can be done in the private sector and what can be done in the public sector may not be as absolute as it is generally believed to be. The policies we advocate can be said to introduce into the operation of the sealed-bid public tender some of the flexibility inherent in negotiations. In particular, the use of reserve prices—that is, of a refusal by government to accept any of the bids if they are all too high (see Chapter 10)—is a way of ensuring that bidders do not build excessively large profit margins into their bids. The use of discriminatory tenders—the offer of a price preference to bidders in a given category (see Chapter 9)—is a way for the government to exploit any observable inherent differences among the bidders in the sealed-bid selection process and to prevent any bidder from exploiting an advantageous position. In the private sector, questions of risk sharing might be addressed in the pre-contract negotiations; risk sharing can be achieved in the context of a sealed-bid tender by using an incentive contract, which makes the payment to the contractor depend not only on his bid but also on his actual production costs (see Chapter 3). Again, a lack of competition among the bidders might be countered in private sector negotiations by a calculated release of information about the bids; in the public sector, use of an incentive contract will have an equivalent effect in stimulating competition and reducing the bids.

Thus the innovations in government-contracting procedures proposed in this study are not inconsistent with the private sector's contracting practices.

3. OUTLINE

The structure of this book is as follows. Chapter 2 explains some background ideas and results from economic theory. Chapter 3 analyses the optimal contract, making use of the concepts introduced in Chapter 2. Chapters 4 and 5 complement the theoretical analysis by investigating the size in practice of the effects identified in the theory. Chapter 4 asks this question: by how much can increasing the amount of competition among firms bidding for a contract lower the price paid by the government? Chapter 5 simulates the optimal contract, provides examples of the government's expected payment for particular projects under differing contract arrangements, and shows how an approximately optimal contract can be computed in practice. Chapter 6 reviews military contracting experience in the United States, drawing lessons from this experience for government contracting in general. Chapter 7 describes the Ontario government's rules covering contracting procedures, while Chapter 8 discusses government procurement policies that explicitly favour domestic suppliers and summarizes a theoretical analysis of the effects of such preferential policies. Chapter 10 discusses the possibilities for privatization: which goods and services are best produced in-house by government agencies, and which can be more efficiently produced by private firms under contract to the government? Finally, Chapter 11 draws together the various strands of the analysis, summarizing the study's results and recommendations.

Although some parts of the analysis focus on the procedures of particular government agencies, other parts are of more general interest. Chapters 2, 3, 9, 10, and 11 provide general analyses of contracting issues; they are relevant to any level of government in any country. Chapters 7 and 8, however, are of relevance to Ontario in particular, while Chapter 6 is about US military contracting. Chapters 4 and 5, which are empirical exercises using mainly Ontario data, provide lessons on the quantitative significance of contracting issues that are of general applicability.

2

Uncertainty and Incentives

Contracts confront both the government agency and the private contractor with uncertainties. The contractor, as an expert in the field, may be better able than the government is to predict the total cost of the project. As a rule, however, not even the contractor can forecast the cost with perfect accuracy: there may be unforeseen changes in labour or raw material costs, or unpredictable difficulties in doing the particular piece of work. To complicate the government's problem, different contractors will perform the same tasks with different degrees of skill, and these differences will not be completely observable.

A government agency that seeks to employ taxpayers' dollars efficiently, by ensuring that its payments to a contractor are as low as is consistent with having the work done satisfactorily, should keep four basic considerations in view. First, the agency should make certain that its procedures for determining which contractor gets the job identify the potential contractor with the lowest cost. Second, the agency should ensure that the contract provides the firm doing the work with incentives to minimize its costs. Third, the agency should recognize that contracting firms may be averse to risk, since a risk-averse firm may be willing to accept a lower profit rate if the agency will absorb some of the project's risk. Fourth, the agency should maintain an auditing scheme of some sort in order to check contractors' claims about costs. This study will investigate all of these aspects of contracting.

The present chapter expounds, in non-technical language, some background ideas and results from economic theory that we shall use later in deriving the characteristics of the optimal contract.

1. COSTS AND PROFITS

In what follows, the terms 'cost' and 'profit' mean *economic cost* and *economic profit*, as opposed to accounting cost and accounting profit. Accounting costs are the dollar amounts actually paid by the firm for labour, raw materials, and so on.

TABLE 2.1
Illustration of the concept of opportunity cost

	If the firm builds the road	If the firm does not build the road
Cost of materials	$10 million	$0
Cost of labour	$40 million	$40 million
Total accounting cost	$50 million	$40 million

Economic costs include both accounting costs and opportunity costs. Opportunity costs measure forgone opportunities; thus the opportunity cost of using a machine in a project is the interest that the money invested in the machine could be earning at the going rate of return, if it were invested elsewhere.

The situation of an oil company in 1979, when oil prices rose precipitously, illustrates the notion of opportunity cost. Oil companies usually keep several months' supply of oil on hand, both as insurance against interruptions of supply or unusually high demand and as a hedge against the normal delays associated with refining. In 1979 the price of oil jumped by about 50 per cent. Thus an oil company that paid $17 for a barrel of oil in early 1979 found itself paying $26 per barrel several months later. A barrel bought at $17 was now worth $26; $26 was the replacement cost, although the accounting cost was just $17. Thus, when the barrel was used, the value given up was $26; this was the opportunity cost of the barrel. The opportunity cost may be greater or smaller than the accounting cost. For example, when gold prices fell in 1981, the opportunity cost of selling gold fell as well.

The opportunity cost of undertaking a government project is the value of projects that cannot be undertaken because of it. Suppose that a firm builds a road for the government instead of building, say, a parking lot for some other client. In this case, the opportunity cost is whatever earnings are lost because the firm did not build the parking lot, plus the costs of the labour and the materials needed to build the road.

Alternatively, suppose that a firm under contract to build a road has no other current project and is required by a union contract to pay its employees whether they work or not. The net cost of labour for the road project firm is zero, since the firm has to pay its employees in any event. Consequently, if the firm is paid anything more than the cost of materials, it will accept the job.

Table 2.1 provides an example of a situation of this kind. If the firm in Table 2.1 is paid anything over $10 million to do the project, it will be in its interest to accept the project. For while the accounting cost of the project is $50 million, the economic cost to the firm—the amount that it must give up in order to undertake the project—is only $10 million. The net cost of the road, the addition to unavoidable expenses, is $10 million, not $50 million.

Economic costs, therefore, include not only the costs of tangibles, such as materials and labour, but also the costs of intangibles, such as profits forgone because the firm's workforce is engaged in the government project. It is economic costs, not accounting cost, that matters to the firm. Economic profit is equal to the difference between total revenue and total economic costs. Economic profit therefore takes account of opportunity costs.

Our analysis will proceed on the assumption, standard in economic theory, that a firm seeks high economic profits. In practice, however, a firm's profit-seeking activities will be conditioned by the extent to which it prefers to avoid risk. The firm might reject the opportunity that would yield, on average, the highest profits if that opportunity involved substantial risk. How can the firm's attitudes towards risk be characterized?

2. UNCERTAINTY

Uncertainty is inherent in any project. The contract between the government and the firm must be written before all the relevant facts are known. There may be unforeseeable increases in the costs of inputs, or unforeseeable difficulties in completing the project. The government, in designing the optimal contract, should therefore take account of how such uncertainties may affect the behaviour of the contracting firm. The firm's behaviour in the face of risk will depend on whether it is *risk neutral* or *risk averse*.

An economic agent is risk neutral if he is indifferent between receiving some amount of money with certainty and taking a gamble that returns on average the same amount of money. An agent who is risk averse will prefer the certain outcome to the gamble. For example, if a risk-averse individual were offered the choice between a sure $100 and a lottery ticket that yielded $200 with 50 per cent probability and nothing with 50 per cent probability, he would choose the $100. A risk-neutral individual, in contrast, would be indifferent between the two choices. The fact that most people buy household and automobile insurance is evidence that most people are risk averse: for the price of the insurance premium, the individual obtains a certain outcome in place of an uncertain outcome.[1] The nature of the optimal government/firm contract is affected by the attitudes toward risk of both the government and the firm.

Are firms risk averse or risk neutral? It can be argued that firms should be less risk averse than individuals. The owners of a firm typically own shares in many other firms as well. Since these firms engage in diverse activities, the uncertainties associated with any one firm are reasonably independent of the

---

1   See Sinn (1983, chap.3) for a discussion of attitudes toward risk. McAfee (1984) provides an explanation for the existence of risk aversion. See also Drèze (1979) and Lippman and McCall (1981).

uncertainties associated with any other firm. These randomnesses tend on average to cancel each other out (in the same way that insurance companies rarely have large net liabilities). Thus the shareholder's ability to diversify his portfolio minimizes the impact on the shareholder of any one firm's earning low profits: varied portfolios of stock are less risky than a single firm's stock.

Nevertheless, it does not follow that the firm will behave risk neutrally. For one thing, the shareholder cannot diversify away all risks: to the extent that different firms' profits tend to move together (in accordance with the business cycle), the shareholder may want the firms in which he owns shares to exhibit some risk aversion. Also, many of the firms that do government business are small and have only a small number of owners; thus the risks that such firms face may be significant to their owners. A second consideration is that if the firm, after gambling and losing, faces bankruptcy, its assets are likely to be sold for less than their true value (because they may have to be sold quickly, without sufficient searching among prospective purchasers). Thus some aversion to large risks may be warranted. Finally, to the extent that a firm, controlled by salaried managers, is run in the interests of the managers rather than the stockholders, the firm's behaviour might reflect the managers' own attitudes towards risks: the failure of a project might result in a manager's losing his job; thus the firm's behaviour might be risk averse. Diversification possibilities are again relevant. The firm might be risk neutral about a project that makes up only a small fraction of its total activities, but it might be risk averse toward a project that is large relative to its total commitments.

The firm's attitude toward risk can be characterized by the notion of the *risk premium*. Consider a simple example of a risky project: a firm has an equal chance of losing amount X or of winning the same amount. The average gain is zero. That is, if the gamble were repeated many times, the firm would, on average, gain nothing and lose nothing. The risk premium is the amount the firm would pay in excess of the average in order to avoid the risk. To put the matter another way, the value of a risk premium is the most one will pay for insurance beyond the cost of the insurance, which is the average outcome.

A risk-neutral firm is one that is just as happy to accept the risk as it is to accept the expected value of the sure thing, so the risk premium for a risk-neutral firm is zero. That is, a risk-neutral firm will pay nothing to avoid the risk. A risk-averse firm will pay some amount (namely, the risk premium) to avoid the risk. Figure 2.1 plots the risk premium for a gamble against the value X. Notice how the line representing the premium curves gently upwards. This movement illustrates the general willingness of risk-averse individuals to pay more than double to avoid the risk when the risk is doubled. The higher curves correspond to greater degrees of risk aversion.

From the government's perspective, the risk premium is the cost of the risk. Because a risk-averse firm will forgo some profits in order to avoid the risk, the government must pay the risk premium if it is to induce the firm to take the risk. For example, suppose that a project will cost either $10,000 or $12,000,

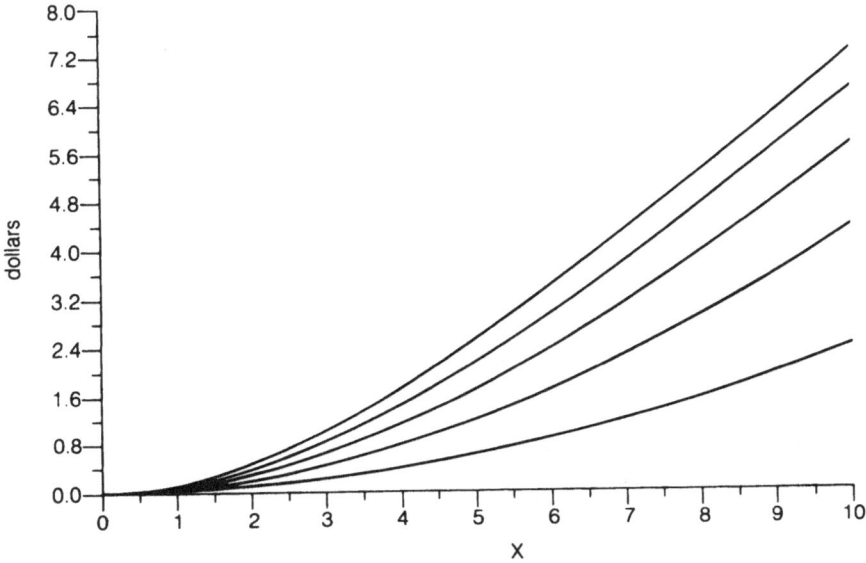

Figure 2.1
Cost of risk of X or −X, each with equal probability, for various degrees of risk aversion

each with equal probability. The average, or expected, cost is $11,000. Suppose that the contracting firm's risk premium for this project is $250. This means that the firm would pay $250 to avoid the risk; that is, to avoid the $10,000 or $12,000 random outcome, it would pay $11,250 with certainty.

Before the firm accepts the contract, it faces no risk. Therefore it must be induced to accept the risk. A payment of $11,250 is a sufficient inducement, for the firm is indifferent between $11,250 with certainty and $10,000 or $12,000 with equal likelihood. Thus, to induce the firm to take such a risk, the government must pay at least $250 beyond the expected cost of $11,000. The $250 represents the increased profits required to make up for the uncertainty. If the government could somehow insure the firm against this risk, it would save $250 on average, because then the firm would have no risk and thus require no risk premium.

Whether firms in fact behave in risk-neutral or risk-averse fashion is an empirical question. Unfortunately, hard evidence relevant to this question is scarce. In an econometric study of firms' attitudes toward risk, Appelbaum and Ullah (1983) were unable to reject the hypothesis that the firms in their sample (the US textile industry) were risk neutral. Scherer has asserted that 'the risk premia needed to lure capital into cyclically volatile industries do not in fact appear to be very large—not more than two or three percentage points on invested capital' (1970: 205). These studies suggest that firms exhibit little, if any, aversion to risk. Contrary but not conclusive evidence comes from a study by Fisher and Hall (1969), who estimated that the risk premia for a sample of large US industrial firms are as high as 8 per cent of stockholders' equity. Since it is likely that the degree of risk aversion varies from firm to firm, the theoretical analysis that follows will allow for both cases: risk-averse firms and risk-neutral firms.

3. GOVERNMENT AS BEARER OF RISK

What the government's attitude toward risk should be is more clear cut. Like the shareholder who owns a diversified portfolio, the government is involved at any time in many independent activities; consequently it may disregard the uncertainties associated with any one activity. Moreover, because the risks associated with any one public project are borne by all of the taxpayers, the cost of risk-bearing is insignificant: an unexpectedly high cost incurred on any one public project will make an insignificant difference to any one citizen's tax bill. For these two reasons (risk pooling and risk spreading), the government should not seek to avoid risk; instead, it is socially efficient for the government to choose its activities in a risk-neutral way. The fact that the government normally self-insures against all risks to its physical assets is evidence that, at least in this respect, its policy is indeed to behave risk neutrally.[2]

Our analysis will assume that governments are, in fact, risk neutral. In practice, however, governments do sometimes exhibit aversion to risk. A government's decisions are made by individuals, who may bear some responsibility for the consequences of their decisions (for example, the outcome of a decision may affect the decision-maker's prospects for promotion). In an environment with uncertainty, decisions must be made before all the relevant facts are known. The correct decision, made by weighing all of the uncertainties, may still leave a significant probability of a bad outcome, especially if the different uncertainties are compared in risk-neutral fashion. Thus a decision that was correct at the outset may result in a bad outcome—the project fails or is unduly costly. When the time comes to evaluate the government official's decision, the situation should be viewed as it appeared when the decision was made, and not with the benefit of hindsight. In other words, it would be wrong to condemn the original decision solely because its ultimate outcome was bad. Unfortunately, this is exactly what the political process tends to do. Failed projects and large cost overruns generate newspaper editorials and parliamentary debates, but these responses often oversimplify the issues and overlook the possibility that the initial decision was the right one given the knowledge

---

2   See, for example, Ontario (1976-83, pp. 45-3-1 to 45-3-3). Arrow and Lind (1970) provide a theoretical defence of the proposition that governments should be risk neutral.

available when it was taken. Thus the political process may force government officials to be averse to risk. This result is costly to society, since, as we have already argued, it is in society's interest that the government be risk neutral. The tendency of the political process to judge decisions on ex post grounds may lead the government to make the wrong decisions: it may take cautious actions when social efficiency requires that the risks be ignored. (Incidentally, this possibility points up one advantage of the much maligned mechanism of decision by committee. Since committee decisions are made collectively, no one individual bears all of the consequences of a bad outcome: thus a committee will tend to be less risk averse than any of its individual members.)

As the numerical examples in the last section demonstrated, if a firm capable of performing some task for the government is risk averse, it might be in the government's interest to absorb some of the risk involved in the performance of the task. The firm cannot be forced to undertake the project: in order to induce the firm to bear the risk, the government must offer it an appropriately high rate of return. Given a risk-averse firm and a risk-neutral government, the total cost to the government of having the task performed would be less if the government bore some of the risk than it would be if the firm were required to bear the entire burden of the risk. In short, if the firm is risk averse, the optimal contract might include some provision for *risk sharing*.

An example is in order. Suppose the government wants to encourage the development of an alternative energy supply. Research is a very risky business, and thus a risk-averse firm would require a very high rate of profit to justify its undertaking such a project. Because the government is involved in many projects, it would not find the risk nearly so significant. Thus, if the government underwrote the risk (by guaranteeing a minimum return, for example), the firm would not require as large an expected profit as it would require if it bore all of the risk itself, and the government's own costs would be correspondingly reduced. In other words, the government would act like an insurance company, insuring the firm against large fluctuations in its profits. In return, the government would receive a reward, the equivalent of the insurance company's premium: the firm would willingly accept a lower payment from the government.

This proposition is illustrated in Figure 2.2. Suppose the risk is an equal probability of winning or losing $10. Let α represent the share of the risk absorbed by the government. For instance, $\alpha = 0$ means that the government bears no risk and the firm bears all of it. If $\alpha = 1$, then the government bears all of the risk. If $\alpha = 1/4$, the government bears a quarter of the risk and the firm bears three-quarters. Figure 2.2 graphs the risk premium against α for various degrees of risk aversion. Note that the savings diminish: as the government takes on extra risk, its returns increase at a lesser rate.

An exception to the presumption that the government is less risk averse than the firm and can therefore lower its payment by absorbing some of the risk sometimes occurs when the government in question is a small municipality.

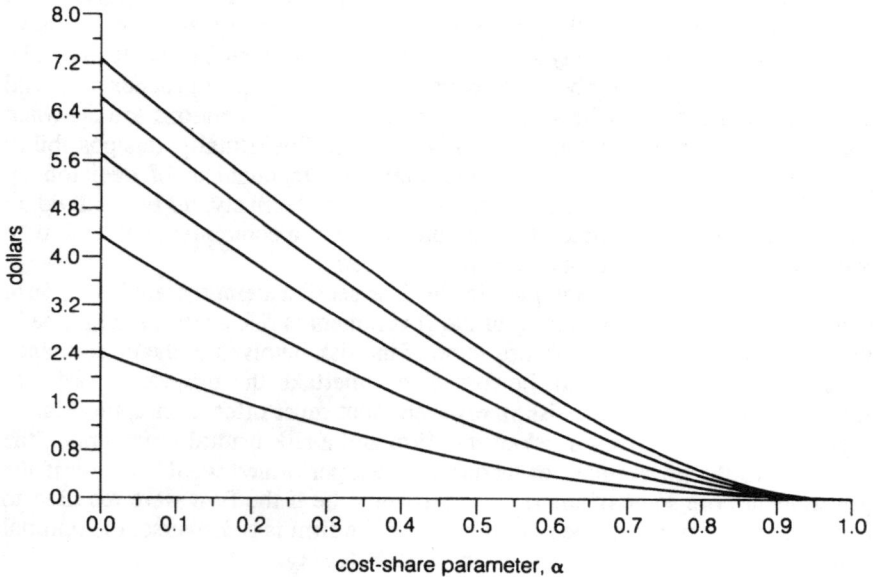

Figure 2.2
Gains from reducing risk, for various degrees of risk aversion

Suppose a municipality contracts with a large firm for a construction project that represents a large fraction of the municipality's budget but only a small fraction of the firm's annual revenue. In this case, it is not in the government's interest to absorb risk on behalf of the firm.

A still better policy than shifting risk from the contractor to the government that is feasible in some circumstances is to reduce uncertainty for both the contractor and the government. Suppose the cost of the project depends on some unpredictable contingency. Suppose moreover (and this is crucial) that both the contractor and the government are able to observe the contingency. Then the government can write the contract so that the amount it pays for the project depends on this contingency. This arrangement reduces the risk the firm must bear and so, to the extent that the firm is risk averse, reduces the price the government must pay. For example, one source of unpredictable cost increases is inflation. If payment is linked to some officially published price index, this particular source of uncertainty is eliminated. We shall discuss this point further in the next chapter.

4. INCENTIVES

The optimal contract should give the firm incentives to make what are, from the government's point of view, the appropriate decisions. The costs that the firm incurs in carrying out the project are, to some extent, within the control of the firm. By exerting effort, the firm can hold down its realized costs. For example, it can, at some cost to itself, search for lower-priced raw materials; or it can resist labour union demands for higher wages; or it can manage its raw materials inventories so that it is not left holding excessive costly stocks. In the other direction, it can artificially inflate its realized costs. For example, it can charge some overhead costs for its other activities to the government project; or it can simply lie when reporting its costs to the government. If the contract is of the cost-plus type, it is obvious that the firm is given no incentive to reduce its costs and no incentive to refrain from inflating its costs.

The propensity of a firm to fail to hold down its costs is an example of *moral hazard*. Moral hazard denotes perverse incentive effects. The term originated in the insurance literature: thus an example of moral hazard occurs if, upon insuring his car against theft, the car owner becomes less careful to prevent theft.

Consider again the government's hypothetical alternative energy project. If the government insures against all of the risk, the firm has no incentive to do the job in an economical manner. Because the firm suffers no ill effects if the final costs are high, it will not take the steps within its power to reduce costs. Consequently it is important to strike a balance between the gains and the losses from risk sharing: the gains were discussed earlier; the losses arise from the lack of incentives to keep project costs down.

Moral hazard, like risk aversion, is an element that the government agency must consider in designing the optimal contract.

5. THE PRINCIPAL-AGENT PROBLEM

The combination of risk sharing and moral hazard constitutes what is known in the economic-theory literature as the *principal/agent problem*.

In the principal/agent problem, the principal employs the agent to perform some task. The agent's output or cost depends on two variables: the agent's level of effort, which the agent chooses, and some random element that is beyond the control of the agent. The agent obviously knows his own effort and also knows the outcome of the random variable. The principal, however, is assumed not to be able to observe this random variable. Therefore the principal cannot, from his observation of the agent's output, deduce what level of effort the agent chose. It is this asymmetry of information that is the crucial element of the principal/agent problem. If the principal were able to observe the agent's effort, he could easily design a reward scheme that induced an appropriate amount of effort from the agent. The optimal reward scheme would pay the agent an amount equal to his marginal product; that is, payment would be proportional to output, as it is under a piece-rate scheme in a labour contract. Given the asymmetry of information, however, the principal cannot disentangle the consequences of the agent's effort from the consequences of the random variable; paying the agent according to his marginal product is unfeasible.

Economists typically solve a principal/agent problem in two stages. (The solution proceeds in the direction opposite to the actual sequence of events.) First, they compute the agent's own best action. This step involves addressing the following question: given a particular contract structure, how must the agent behave to promote his own best interest? The second step is to identify the optimal contract structure. The principal, being able to solve the first stage of the problem, can predict the agent's response to any particular contract design. Thus the principal can choose the contract that is best from his point of view.[3]

A particular version of the general principal/agent problem is solved in Chapters 3 and 4. In this version, the government (or principal) designs a contract that, on average, minimizes the amount paid to the contractor (or agent). In order to find this optimal contract, the government must be able to predict the firm's actions in response to the contract: this exercise requires it to consider both the risk-sharing effect and the moral-hazard effect.

6. BIDDING

In the standard principal/agent problem, there is a particular agent who performs the task for the principal. In the case of government/firm contracting, however, an additional element is present: the government (the principal) is able to choose one particular firm (agent) from a set of possible firms (potential agents). The main theoretical innovation of Chapters 3 and 4 is to introduce the bidding for and the awarding of contracts into the principal/agent framework.

The firms seeking the job submit bids, on the basis of which the government selects one firm. Suppose that each of the firms would incur different costs in performing the task. If the selection rule is to choose the lowest bidder, then the government should ensure that the bidding mechanism induces the lowest-cost firm to bid lowest, so that the correct firm is selected. The government may also wish to encourage competition among the firms in the bidding process, so that the bids are driven down. The more competition there is at the bidding stage, the less the government actually pays to have the task performed.

The process of bidding for the right to perform a task is, in its structure, very similar to the process of bidding to buy a particular item. Bidding has been modelled in the recent economic-theory literature as a question of optimal auction design.

Suppose the owner of a unique item (a work of art, for example) wishes to

---

3   For a survey of the principal/agent problem, see MacDonald (1984); see also the analyses of Gjesdal (1982), Grossman and Hart (1983), Harris and Raviv (1979), Harris and Townsend (1985), Holmström (1979), Rogerson (1983), Shavell (1979), and Townsend (1979).

sell it. There are several potential buyers. Since the item is unique, its price, unlike the price of wheat or the price of gold, cannot be established by supply and demand. The uniqueness of the item confers some monopoly power on its owner; he can choose the procedure by which the item is sold. Two types of auction are in common use: the first-price sealed-bid auction, in which the potential buyers submit sealed bids and the bidder who submits the highest bid receives the item and pays the amount he bid; and the English auction, in which an auctioneer calls successively higher prices until only one bidder remains, who then pays the price he bid and receives the item. The crucial difference between the two types of auction is the amount of information the bidders have about others' bids: potential buyers in a sealed-bid auction must guess how much the others have bid, while in an English auction all bids are observed. The first-price sealed-bid auction is used when a government sells the mineral rights on government-owned land; it is also used in the weekly treasury bill auction in New York. The English auction is usually used in selling artwork, antiques, or livestock. How should the owner organize the selling process to his own best advantage? Which of the two types of auction will, on average, generate the highest price for the item?

An essentially identical problem arises when a buyer wishes to acquire a unique item from one of several potential suppliers. For example, the government may wish to procure a fleet of cars or certain office equipment. The buyer calls for tenders from the potential sellers. In principle, the tendering process can be organized like either a sealed-bid auction or an English auction: that is, either the buyer chooses the lowest tender from a set of sealed-bid tenders or an auctioneer calls successively lower prices until only one interested bidder remains. Which of these two approaches results in a lower payment by the buyer?

Comparing the prices that result from the two types of auction yields a surprising conclusion. It can be shown that, if all of the potential suppliers are risk neutral, then under reasonably general conditions the buyer will be indifferent between the two types of tendering procedure. On average, each type will result in the same price being paid for the item.[4]

This equivalence between the two types of tendering procedures breaks down if the suppliers are risk averse. With risk-averse suppliers, the buyer's expected payment is lower under the sealed-bid tender than it is under the English tender. Thus if the suppliers are risk averse, or if the buyer does not

---

4   These results are from Holt (1980), Harris and Raviv (1981), Myerson (1981), Riley and Samuelson (1981), Matthews (1983), and Maskin and Riley (1984). See these papers for precise statements of the underlying assumptions and for proofs of the results. The conclusions offered in this and the subsequent paragraphs depend on the assumptions that each potential supplier knows his own expected cost for the project and that the suppliers' expected costs are statistically independent — see Milgrom and Weber (1982). On auctions in practice, see Cassady (1967), Crommelin, Pearse, and Scott (1978), and Mead (1967).

know whether the suppliers are risk averse or risk neutral, the buyer should use the sealed-bid tendering process.

To understand why the sealed-bid tender results in a lower expected price than does the English tender when suppliers are risk averse, note that there is not usually a large number of bidders. Thus the competition among bidders is not usually fierce enough to eliminate all of the profits of the winner. The winner therefore expects to earn a positive profit; consequently each potential supplier wishes to win the tender. Recall that risk-averse people behave more cautiously in the face of uncertainty than do risk-neutral people. The difference between the sealed-bid tender and the English tender is a difference in the amount of uncertainty the bidders face. In the English tender, each bidder knows how much the others have bid. In the sealed-bid tender, each bidder can only guess about others' bids. Thus there is more uncertainty in the sealed-bid tender than there is in the English tender. This extra uncertainty is what causes the winner's bid to be lower in the sealed-bid tender than it is in the English tender, given that the suppliers are risk averse. Because he does not know how low the others have bid in a sealed-bid tender, a risk-averse supplier will tend to lower his bid, thereby reducing the profit he earns if he wins but increasing the probability that he will win. The risk-averse supplier prefers to reduce his uncertainty; lowering his bid makes it less likely that he will lose the sealed-bid tender.

If there are a great many potential suppliers, then even if the suppliers are risk averse the difference between the price under the sealed-bid tender and the price under the English tender disappears. With a very large number of bidders, there is so much bidding competition that the profits of the winner are driven to zero (as in the standard model of perfect competition in elementary economic theory). Consequently potential suppliers are indifferent between winning and losing the bidding process. Risk aversion does not cause the potential suppliers to shade their bids in the sealed-bid tender. The expected price is the same under each type of tendering process.

This last result suggests a further result. Consider a sealed-bid tender in which there are only a few bidders, so that the bidding competition does not eliminate all of the winner's economic profits. Adding one extra bidder will increase the amount of bidding competition, causing each bidder to bid somewhat lower. Thus the more bidders there are, the lower are the bids and therefore the lower is the price ultimately paid by the buyer. This conclusion suggests that it is in the buyer's interest to stimulate bidding competition by encouraging as many potential suppliers as possible to submit bids.

It is possible to design hypothetical tendering procedures that produce still better results for the buyer than the sealed-bid tender produces if the suppliers are risk averse. In the hypothetical optimal tender, risk is shifted from the low bidders to the high bidders. The buyer achieves this shift by refusing to accept extremely high bids, by requiring bidders who bid sufficiently high to pay a penalty if they lose, and by subsidizing the bidders who bid relatively low but lose.[5] These policies increase the suppliers' fear of losing, thereby increasing bidding competition and lowering the price paid by the buyer. However, because of the computational complexity of this tendering process, and because considerations of equity may rule out forcing losers to pay in government tenders, we shall not discuss the process further in this study.

7. COLLUSION IN BIDDING

In order to produce bids for the performance of a given task, the government requests bids for the project from any firms capable of performing it. Alternatively, the government advertises the project and firms respond if they find it profitable. The theory we develop in this study assumes that the firms bid in a non-cooperative manner; that is, they do not collude. This means, for example, that the firms do not somehow come to an agreement to raise all of their bids. There are three justifications for this assumption. First, such collusion is illegal. Second, the colluding firms must solve the difficult problem of dividing the spoils: which firm is to be allowed to win any particular contract? Third, collusion contains the seeds of its own destruction: the high profits earned in an industry whose members are successfully colluding attract new firms to the industry; the competition from these new entrants will tend to destroy the collusive arrangements.

Although collusive arrangements eventually break down, they often persist for a number of years. Thus collusion might in some instances be a serious short-term problem for the government. It is not possible to design a contract that makes collusion unprofitable; any contract is susceptible to manipulation by joint action of the bidders. Thus the optimal contract proposed in Chapter 3 does not solve the problem of collusion.

However, there are actions that the government can take to make collusion difficult. Prosecution under anti-combines legislation is one possibility; Adam Smith recognized over 200 years ago the most important sign of the existence of collusion: 'People of the same trade seldom meet together, even for merriment or diversion, but the conversation ends in a conspiracy against the public, or in some contrivance to raise prices' (Smith 1976: I, 144). The government can hinder the growth of collusion by encouraging new firms to enter the industry; again, new entrants will tend to break up any existing collusive arrangements. Moreover, as we have already suggested, even in the absence of collusion an increase in the number of bidders tends to lower the government's expected costs, since it increases competition among the bidders and drives their bids down. A fruitful way of fostering entry and, therefore, bidding competition is to provide information about contracting methods and technologies.

5 For details, see Maskin and Riley (1984), Matthews (1983, 1984), and Moore (1984). See Chapter 10, section 5, and McAfee and McMillan (1985) for another way of improving on the simple sealed-bid auctioning.

8. THE SOCIAL VALUE OF EXPENDITURE SAVINGS

This study will suggest ways in which government expenditure can be reduced without sacrificing government programs. The significance of reducing government expenditure and therefore reducing the need for tax revenue is obvious, especially if the reduction can be achieved without losing any of the benefits from government activity. The gain to society, however, from any tax reduction is greater than just the number of tax dollars saved. Each dollar by which taxation is reduced results in more than a dollar's worth of increase in social welfare.

Any type of taxation creates a distortion. The income tax, for example, distorts the choice between labour and leisure. The income tax creates perverse incentives: since the worker does not keep the entire amount of any extra income he earns from working harder, he works less hard than he would in the absence of the tax. A sales tax distorts consumers' spending patterns, since it tends to bias consumption in the direction of commodities that are not taxed or that are less heavily taxed. It does not follow from these observations that such taxes should not exist: if the government is to function, it must raise revenue somehow. But it does follow that each extra dollar in tax revenue imposes a loss on society as a whole of more than one dollar.

Ballard, Shoven, and Whalley (1985) have estimated the size of this effect for the United States, and it seems likely that similar figures would apply to Canada and other modern mixed economies. According to this estimate, each extra dollar raised in income tax generates distortions that impose an extra cost on society as a whole of between $1.17 and $1.56. To put this another way, the estimated value to society of reducing taxes is between 17 per cent and 56 per cent more than the size of the tax reduction.[6]

---

6 See also Campbell (1975), Starrett (1983), and Stuart (1984).

3

The Optimal Contract

The question examined in this chapter is: how can a given level of government services be produced at the least cost? (The question of how this level of government services should be determined is outside the scope of the present study.) We shall derive the form of the optimal government/firm contract theoretically, taking into account four effects: the bidding competition effect, the risk-sharing effect, the moral-hazard effect, and the cost-padding effect.

Our analysis will consider three types of contract: the *fixed-price contract* (sometimes called a 'lump-sum' contract), the *cost-plus contract* (also called a 'force-account' contract), and the *incentive contract*. Under a fixed-price contract, the government's payment to the contractor is simply the amount of the firm's bid. Thus the government's payment is the same whatever the actual costs to the firm of completing the task, while the firm's profits vary inversely with the costs. Under a cost-plus contract, the government pays the firm a fixed fee plus the firm's costs. In this case, the government's payment varies directly with the costs, while the firm's profits are guaranteed. The incentive contract combines features of the cost-plus contract and the fixed-price contract: the government's payment depends on both the firm's bid and the firm's actual costs. If the actual costs exceed the bid, then part of the cost overrun is paid by the firm and part by the government, according to a pre-arranged sharing ratio. If the costs are less than the bid, the government and the firm share the savings. Thus both the government's payment and the firm's profits vary with the costs actually incurred.

Depending on the particular features of the project to be undertaken, any one of these three contract types could be optimal. This chapter seeks to characterize the conditions under which these contract types are optimal and, in the case of the incentive contract, to derive a way of computing the optimal sharing ratio for cost overruns and underruns.

In order to keep the discussion non-technical, we shall not state our underlying assumptions precisely or attempt to prove our results in this chapter. A rigorous analysis of the optimal contract, with proofs of the results discussed here, appears in McAfee and McMillan (1986).

1. THE LINEAR CONTRACT

Under a fixed-price contract, the government pays the firm a fixed sum of money upon completion of the project. The amount paid is the firm's bid. Thus, if the successful firm's bid is b, the government pays it an amount τ, where

(1) $\tau = b$.

Under a cost-plus contract, the government's payment covers realized costs. Thus, if the firm incurs total costs (including opportunity costs) of c, the payment from government to firm, τ, is either

(2) $\tau = c + \theta b$

or

(3) $\tau = (1 + \theta)c$,

where θ represents the profit rate. Under what is called a 'cost plus fixed fee' contract (equation 2), profit is computed as a percentage of the bid. Thus the firm's profit is the same regardless of its costs, and profit as a fraction of costs declines as costs increase. Under what is called a 'cost plus percentage fee' contract (equation 3) profit is computed as a percentage of true costs: profit increases as costs increase. However, this study will give little attention to the distinctions between the different types of cost-plus contract, since, as we shall argue below, no cost-plus contract can be optimal from the government's point of view.

Payments under an incentive contract depend not only on the bid, like payments under a fixed-price contract, but also on the realized costs, like payments under a cost-plus contract. Specifically, if the firm's costs exceed its bid, the firm is responsible for some fraction of the cost overrun. Similarly, if the firm succeeds in holding its costs below its bid, the firm is paid a fraction of the cost underrun. Let $1 - \alpha$ represent the fraction of any cost overrun or cost underrun that accrues to the firm. Under an incentive contract, the payment from government to firm is

(4) $\tau = b + \alpha(c - b)$.

The government chooses the size of the parameter α, which we shall call the *cost-share parameter*.

Consider, for example, a road-building project for which the selected firm's bid was $50 million. If the cost-share parameter is 0.8 (this is a typical number for US defence contracts), the government must pay the firm 0.2 x $50 million, or $10 million, plus 80 per cent of the costs actually incurred. If the actual costs equal the bid, then the government pays the bid. Suppose a cost overrun occurs, and final costs are $60 million. Then the government must pay 80 per cent of this amount for a total cost of $10 million + (0.8 x $60 million), or $58 million. That is, the government shares in the cost overrun, taking 80 per cent, or $8 million, of it. Finally, suppose a cost underrun occurs, and actual costs are $40 million. In this case, the government pays $42 million. The government thus shares in the cost reduction, by saving $8 million, in the same way as it shared in the cost overrun.

If $\alpha = 0$ in equation 4, the contract reduces to a fixed-price contract (equation 1). If $\alpha = 1$ in equation 4, the contract becomes essentially—as we shall show later in this chapter—a cost-plus contract of the type described by equation 3. Thus the spectrum of contracts, fixed-price through incentive to cost-plus, is traced by increasing the cost-share parameter α from zero to one. An increase in the cost-share parameter increases the government's share in the risk of the project. When $\alpha = 0.8$, as in the example above, it bears 80 per cent of the risk; and so on. As we shall see, however, risk-bearing is not the only role of the cost-share parameter.

Since the government chooses the value of the cost-share parameter, α, the problem of the optimal design of government contracts is the problem of determining the value of α that will, on average, minimize the government's payments. Our analysis derives both the conditions under which a fixed-price contract is optimal and those under which an incentive contract is optimal. It also develops a method for determining the optimal value of the cost-share parameter in those cases in which an incentive contract is optimal.

2. REALIZED COSTS

In the model developed in this chapter, the total cost that a contracting firm reports to the government may have up to four components.

First, there is the expected cost of the project, which reflects that particular firm's efficiency in doing the work. It must be stressed that the expected cost includes all opportunity costs, as defined in the previous chapter. Thus the cost to the firm of undertaking a government project includes a valuation of the activities the firm must forgo in order to undertake the government project. If the economy is booming, so that the firm has many profitable alternatives to the government project, then the costs to the firm of undertaking the government project (given the economist's definition of cost) will be high. If the economy is slack, the cost to the firm of doing government work will be low. As we shall see, differences in firms' costs caused by differences in their alternative opportunities will be reflected in the firms' bids. Thus if one of two firms with identical machinery and labour forces has better alternative opportunities than the other, it will bid higher.

The second component of production cost in our model is a random variable that represents unpredictable costs. The level of this random variable is observed by the firm after the firm has been selected, but cannot be accurately observed by the government. This variable represents the vagaries of the project: the peculiarities of a particular construction site, unforeseeable technological difficulties, delays caused by bad weather or accidents, unforeseen increases in labour or interest costs.

The third component of the contracting firm's cost is the cost of any cost-reducing activity that the firm may undertake. Thus the firm might lower its total costs by obtaining lower input prices or by scheduling construction so that materials arrive as they are needed. Our model assumes that cost-reducing activity is itself costly to the firm, and that the firm cannot charge these costs to the project. (Any cost-reducing innovation that can be charged to the project could, for the purposes of modelling, be directly embedded in the first of the cost components, the expected cost.) Since cost-reducing activities require costly effort, they will not be undertaken without the appropriate incentives. (We shall discuss cost-reduction activities and their quantitative significance in detail in Chapter 5.)

Fourth, the firm might fraudulently inflate its reported costs. A firm engaged in cost padding might charge the fixed costs of other projects to the government project, charge for materials not used, or charge a higher price for materials than it actually paid. If the government audits contracting firms' accounts, then the firm runs a risk in padding its costs—a risk that it will take into account in making its cost-reporting decisions. It might, however, still be in the firm's interest to do some cost padding.

In our model, the government, being risk neutral, will design contracts with a view to minimizing, on average, its payment to contracting firms. (The qualification 'on average' is necessary because the government must operate under some irremovable uncertainty: it can never accurately learn about the second, random component of a firm's total costs.) In this context, designing a contract means choosing a value between zero and one for the parameter α in equation 4.

3. THE POTENTIAL CONTRACTORS' OPTIMIZATION

Before a contract is awarded, several potential contractors submit sealed bids (denoted b in equation 4). The government's first task is to design a bidding process that distinguishes between high-cost and low-cost firms. Different firms will have different capabilities for performing the particular task. Every firm has better information about its own costs than the government has. Since the government has no basis for its choice except the firms' bids, is it possible that, by understating its true costs in the bidding, a firm will increase its chances of being selected? In other words, can it happen that, by choosing the firm that bids lowest, the government mistakenly chooses a high-cost firm?

In McAfee and McMillan (1986), the bidding process is modelled as a non-cooperative game and it is shown that it is a simple matter for the government to ensure that it selects the most efficient firm. In the case of a fixed-price contract or an incentive contract (that is, where α is strictly less than 1), the lower any firm expects its production costs to be, the lower it will bid. Thus the government, in selecting the lowest bidder, does in fact select the most efficient firm for the job.

In the case of a cost-plus contract ($\alpha = 1$), this argument breaks down. Because the firm's actual costs are completely covered by the government, the firm's expected costs are irrelevant to the determination of its bid. Lower-cost firms will not necessarily bid lower; bids fail to reveal relative expected costs. Thus there is no reason to suppose that, in selecting the lowest bidder, the government selects the firm with the lowest expected costs.

The size of the cost-share parameter determines the intensity of the competition among the bidding firms. If the contract is a fixed-price contract ($\alpha = 0$), each firm will bid high, since its bid, if successful, will have to entirely cover its costs. Under a cost-plus contract ($\alpha = 1$), the government will completely cover the actual costs; therefore each firm can ignore its expected costs in deciding its bid and will bid low in order to win the contract. With an incentive contract (α between 0 and 1), the larger α is, the lower each firm's bid will be. This is because the correspondence between a firm's production cost and the size of its bid diminishes as α increases: the greater is the proportion of production costs absorbed by the government, the less production costs matter to the firm when it decides its bid. What determines how large a profit margin a firm builds into its bid is how close the next-lowest-cost firm's cost is to its own cost. Increasing α has the same effect as reducing the difference between different firms' production costs; it makes the firms bid lower because they face closer competition from their rivals. The lower the bids are, the lower is the government's expected payment. We shall call this effect of the cost-share parameter α on the firms' bids the *bidding-competition effect*.

To see how the bidding competition effect works, consider the case of two firms bidding for a given job. Firm 1 has costs of $100, while firm 2 has costs of $200. If firm 1 knows firm 2's costs, it will bid $199.99 to do the job, for any higher bid would allow firm 2 to undercut firm 1. Now suppose the government sets α at 0.5. Firm 2 can now bid $100 and break even if it wins, for it will be paid its bid plus half of its costs of $200, or a total of $200. In this case, firm 1 must bid no more than $99.99 in order to win, and it has no reason to bid less. Consequently the government's payment is $149.99—firm 1's bid of $99.99 plus half of the firm's costs of $100. Thus the government's cost with α set at 0.5 is $50 less than it would have been under a fixed-price contract.

In this example the successful firm is risk neutral. If the selected firm is risk averse, the government's choice of a value for the cost-share parameter, α, has a second effect on the firm's actions. The greater is the risk that the government imposes on a risk-averse firm, the higher are the profits that the government must, on average, allow the firm to earn; otherwise, the firm will not accept the contract. In other words, the government must pay a price, in the form of a higher expected payment to the firm, for any risk it shifts from itself to the firm. If the contract is a cost-plus contract ($\alpha = 1$), the government bears all of the risk of unpredictable cost increases and the firm bears none. If the contract is a fixed-price contract ($\alpha = 0$), the firm bears all of the risk and the government bears none. Consequently a risk-averse firm will expect a higher rate of return on a fixed-price contract than on a cost-plus contract. For incentive contracts (where the value of α is between 0 and 1), the larger α is, the lower is the government's expected payment. We shall call this effect of the government's choice of α on the firm's behaviour the *risk-sharing effect*. The risk-sharing effect reinforces the bidding competition effect.

The two effects of the cost-share parameter, α, on cost-control activity, the *moral-hazard effect* and the *cost-padding effect*, work in the opposite direction. Under a fixed-price contract ($\alpha = 0$), the firm has a strong incentive to seek ways of lowering costs and no incentive to pad costs, since the firm is itself responsible for any excess costs. Under a cost-plus contract ($\alpha = 1$), the firm has no incentive to exert effort to lower costs and a strong incentive to pad costs, since any excess costs will be covered by government. Under an incentive contract (α between 0 and 1), the firm chooses its optimal levels of cost-reducing activity and cost-padding activity. It does this by equating the marginal return from each of these activities to its marginal cost. The firm's optimal level of each activity is determined by the size of the cost-share parameter chosen by the government. The smaller α is (that is, the closer the contract is to a fixed-price contract), the more cost-reducing activity and the less cost-padding activity the firm undertakes.[1]

Thus the government's choice of the optimal cost-share parameter involves a tradeoff. The larger the parameter α is, the lower is the government's expected payment because of the risk-sharing and bidding-competition effects, but the higher is the government's expected payment because of the moral-hazard and cost-padding effects.

---

1 Recall the nature of the firm's costs and benefits from cost-reduction and cost-padding activities. Under a fixed-price contract or incentive contract, the firm keeps part or all of any savings in costs it achieves. But in order to achieve these savings, it must incur some cost that it cannot charge the government project. For example, the firm may lower its cost by eliminating excess personnel or equipment; the cost to the firm is lower sales and therefore lower profits in the future. Under a cost-plus contract, the government bears all or part of the costs to the firm of undertaking the project. Thus it might pay the firm to artificially inflate its costs —by overcharging the government for inputs used, for example, or by charging the fixed costs of other projects to the government project. The cost to the firm of such activities arises from the risks that they entail: if the overcharging is detected in an audit, the firm may suffer the imposition of a heavy fine or a loss of its chance to win future government contracts.

4. THE GOVERNMENT'S OPTIMIZATION

The government can itself go through the computations of the firm as we have just described them. Therefore it can, on average, predict the response of a firm to the government's choice of contract. (Again, the qualification 'on average' is required because the government never has as much information as the firm.)The government can use this knowledge about the firm's responses in designing its optimal contract.

The government wishes to choose the level of the cost-share parameter, α, that minimizes, on average, the amount it must pay to the firm. Suppose the government has set α at some arbitrary level. Can it, by changing α, reduce its payments on average? An increase in α brings both a benefit and a cost to the government: because of the risk-sharing effect and the bidding-competition effect it tends to reduce the government's payment; but because of the moral-hazard effect and the cost-padding effect it tends to increase the government's payment. Let the term 'marginal benefit' (MB) denote the rate at which the government's expected payment declines as α rises, owing to risk aversion and

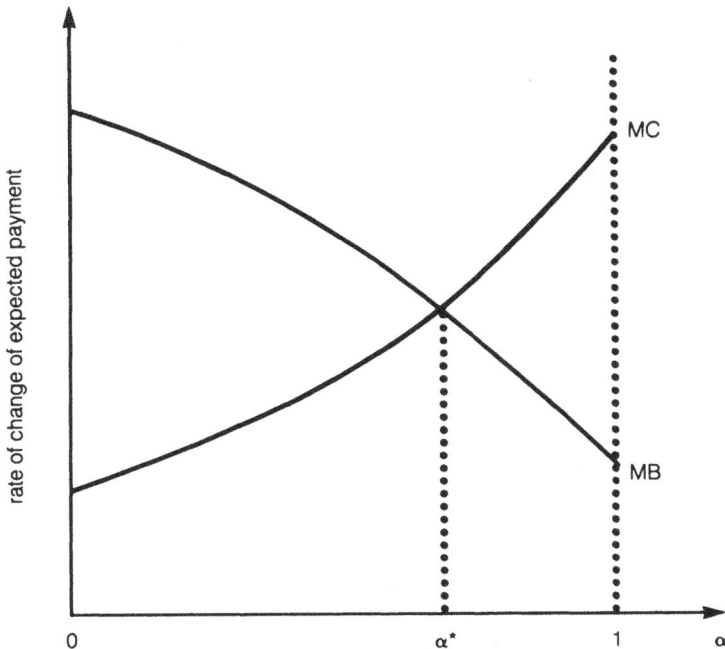

Figure 3.1
Optimal choice of cost-share parameter. The cost of increasing α results from decreased incentive to control costs and increased incentive to defraud. The benefit results from increased bidding competition and increased risk sharing.

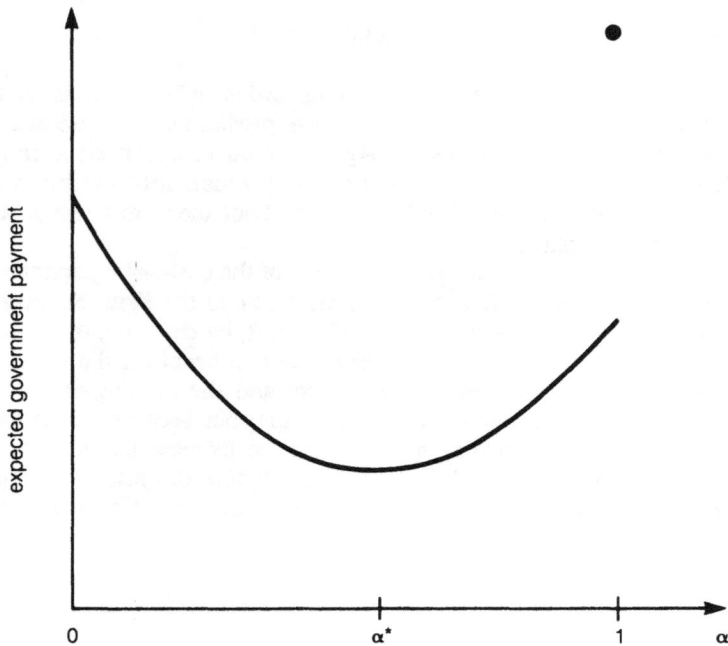

Figure 3.2
Variation of expected government payment with cost-share parameter

bid competition. Let the term 'marginal cost' (MC) denote the rate at which the government's expected payment rises as α increases, owing to moral hazard and cost padding. Then, as Figure 3.1 shows, the optimal value of the cost-share parameter, α^*, is found by equating marginal benefit to marginal cost. Any increase in α beyond α^* yields an increase in expected payment (the result of reduced incentives for cost control by the firm) that is larger than the concomitant decrease in expected payment (the result of increased risk sharing and bidding competition). The choice of a level of α below α^* fails to exploit fully the risk-aversion and bidding-competition effects.

If the value α^* at which the marginal-cost curve and the marginal-benefit curve intersect is less than zero, then the optimal value of α is zero and a fixed-price contract is prescribed. If α^* lies between 0 and 1, then the best contract is an incentive contract with cost-share parameter α^*.

Figure 3.2 presents the information in Figure 3.1 in another way. Varying the cost-share parameter, α, varies the government's expected payment. The optimal cost-share parameter, α^*, corresponds to the minimum point of Figure 3.2: at this point, the government's expected payment reaches its lowest possible value. Note a peculiarity of the expected-government-payment curve: when α

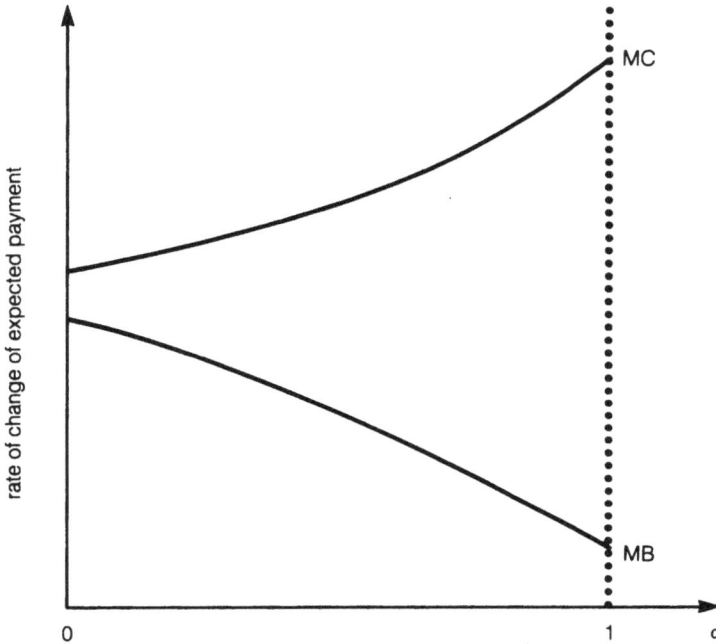

Figure 3.3
Optimal choice of cost-share parameter: fixed-price contract optimal

reaches 1, the curve jumps upward; there is a discontinuity when α becomes equal to 1. This discontinuity reflects the drawback of the cost-plus contract that we have already mentioned. As long as α is strictly less than 1, firms must take account of their expected production costs when they decide how low to bid. As a result, the lowest-cost firm bids lowest and the government, in choosing the lowest bidder, chooses the most efficient firm. When α is equal to 1, however (that is, when the contract is a cost-plus contract), expected production cost is irrelevant to the decision about size of bid. Any firm can afford to submit a bid that is below its expected production cost because it knows that its actual costs, whatever they turn out to be, will be covered by the government. Bids therefore fail to reveal relative expected costs; the government will select the most efficient firm only by accident. Choosing the lowest bidder for a cost-plus contract is equivalent to choosing a firm at random. Hence the amount the government can expect to pay on the average takes a sudden jump upwards when α becomes equal to 1.

Figures 3.1 and 3.2 beg an important question: they are drawn in such a way that the optimal cost-share parameter is between 0 and 1, so that the optimal

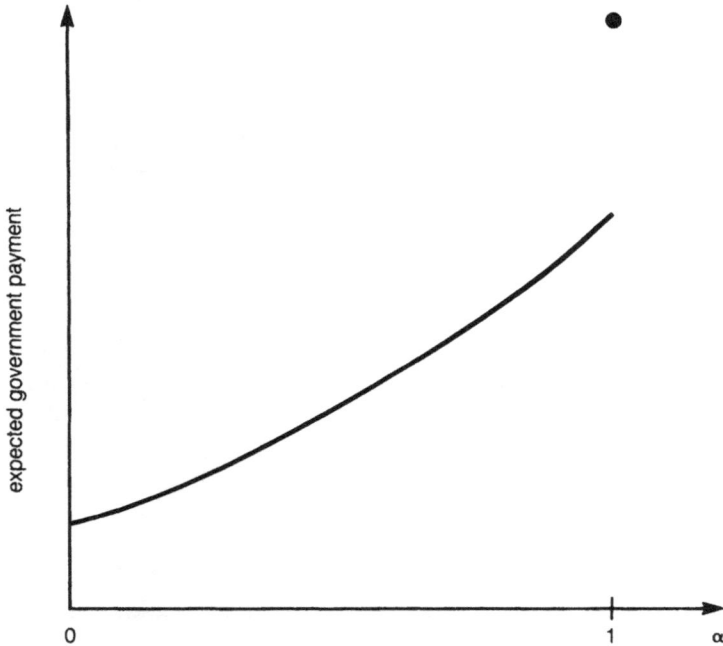

Figure 3.4
Variation of expected government payment with cost-share parameter:
fixed-price contract optimal

contract is an incentive contract. This need not be the case. Figures 3.3 and 3.4, which correspond respectively to Figures 3.1 and 3.2, depict an alternative possibility. In Figure 3.3, the marginal benefit and marginal cost curves never cross: the marginal cost of increasing α always exceeds the marginal benefit. The cost-share parameter α should therefore be set at its minimum possible level, which is 0. In other words, a fixed-price contract is optimal. Figure 3.4 represents the same situation: the lowest point on the curve that represents the government's expected payment is attained when α is 0.

The marginal-benefit and marginal-cost curves depicted in Figures 3.1 and 3.3 and the government's expected payment curve depicted in Figures 3.2 and 3.4 are characterized in detail in McAfee and McMillan (1986). The results of that analysis can be summarized as follows.

5. COST-PLUS AND FIXED-PRICE CONTRACTS

Which type of contract is optimal in any particular case depends on such factors as the amount of uncertainty associated with the project, the variance of the bidders' expected costs, the amount of competition in bidding, the ability and willingness of the selected firm to hold down its costs, and the bidding firms' attitudes towards risk.[2]

The fixed-price contract is optimal if and only if (a) the bidders are all risk neutral and (b) either all bidders have the same expected costs or there are so many bidders that one extra bidder would not noticeably lower the probability of any particular firm's submitting the lowest bid. The reason why a fixed-price contract is optimal only under these conditions can be understood by recalling the fundamental tradeoff involved in fixed-price contract design. The advantage of a fixed-price contract is that it gives the contractor strong incentives to seek out ways of reducing costs and to abstain from padding costs. Its disadvantages are that it fails to induce strong competition at the bidding stage and requires the selected firm to bear all the risk of unpredictable cost increases. These disadvantages disappear only when the conditions (a) and (b) are satisfied. If the firms are risk neutral, then shifting all of the project's risk to the firm does not raise the cost of the contract to the government. If there are many bidders, or if all of the bidders have the same expected costs, then the maximum possible amount of competition in bidding is already assured; consequently there is no need to use the terms of the contract to stimulate bidding competition.

The fixed-price contract is the most common form of government contract. Our theoretical analysis has shown that unless conditions (a) and (b) are both satisfied a fixed-price contract is suboptimal; that is, it costs the government more than would a contract that stimulated bidding competition and allowed some risk sharing. In practice, these conditions are not often met. Frequently, only a few firms submit bids. There is usually a spread in the values of the bids submitted, which indicates that the bidders have different expected costs. Indeed, it is unlikely that any two firms will have the same costs for a given project. For two firms to have identical costs, they would have to have not only identical capabilities for doing the work, but also identical alternative work opportunities.

The pure cost-plus contract is never optimal if there is more than one potential contractor. Because the cost-plus contract does not require the contractor to bear any of the risk, it does succeed in stimulating strong bidding competition. In fact, the fault of the cost-plus contract is that it induces so much bidding competition that the lowest-cost firm will not necessarily submit the lowest bid. The bidding process fails to reveal relative expected costs. If more than one firm bids, then it is likely that the government will select the wrong firm.

Notice that this argument is different from the standard objection to cost-plus contracts: namely that a cost-plus contract gives the firm no incentive to

---

2   Recall that a firm is said to be risk neutral if it would be indifferent between, for example, a project that yielded a profit of $500 with certainty and a project that yielded a loss of $4,000 with 50 per cent probability and a profit of $5,000 with 50 per cent probability. If the possible profit was any amount more than $5,000, the risk-neutral firm would definitely choose the gamble. A firm is said to be risk averse if, in the example given, it would choose the certain alternative.

keep its costs low. In practice, the firm's cost-controlling activity can to some extent be monitored by the government: there is a limit to how much the contractor's costs can be inflated. The fact that the cost-plus contract defeats the very purpose of competitive bidding is a more fundamental objection to its use.

While a pure cost-plus contract cannot be optimal if there is more than one potential contractor, in some circumstances a contract very close to cost-plus is optimal. Such a contract would be an incentive contract with a cost-share parameter α close to 1, so that almost all of any cost overrun would be borne by the government. Provided the firm bears some share, however small, of a cost overrun, the bidding competition will reveal the firm with the lowest expected cost. The optimal contract tends to be close to a cost-plus contract if the following conditions are met: the number of bidders is small; bidders' expected costs vary widely; the returns to cost-reduction activity diminish substantially; bidders are markedly risk averse; there are severe penalties for fraud. In these cases, $\alpha = 0.9$ or 0.99, say, might be a good choice.

It is sometimes claimed that the use of cost-plus contracts is justified in the case of projects that involve extreme uncertainty, such as research and development projects. The theoretical analysis in Chapter 4 shows that this claim is not correct. An increase in the riskiness of the outcome does tend to push the optimal incentive contract in the direction of the cost-plus contract. But the optimal contract must give the firms incentives to reveal their expected costs in their bidding, and these incentives will be absent if the contract requires the government to cover completely the selected firm's actual costs.

6. THE INCENTIVE CONTRACT

If, as is likely to be the case, the conditions under which a fixed-price contract is optimal are not met, then the optimal type of contract is the incentive contract. If the government decides to use an incentive contract, it must then decide what value (between 0 and 1) to assign to the cost-share parameter α. We have already indicated the conditions under which the optimal value of α will tend to be large. If the following conditions are met, the optimal cost-share parameter will tend to be small: the spread in the bidders' expected costs is small; the number of bidders is large; the degree of unpredictable fluctuation in the costs of doing the work is small; the returns to cost-reducing activity diminish only slightly; and the penalty for fraud is small.

The study will therefore recommend that government make use of incentive contracts under certain circumstances, which we shall specify. A likely objection to this recommendation is that it would not be practicable for a government to collect the information and carry out the complicated computations necessary for the implementation of an incentive contract. This objection is easily countered by reference to military contracting experience in the United States. As we shall show in Chapter 5, incentive contracts are used successfully, and to an increasing extent, in US defence contracting.

However, our recommendations go one step further than the US practice. In the US defence contracts, the cost-share parameter appears to be determined in an unsystematic way. We propose, in Chapter 5, a formula for computing the optimal value of the cost-share parameter.

There is an analogy between the incentive contract and remuneration arrangements often used in private sector contracts, such as royalties and commissions. Thus a contract between a publisher and an author usually specifies a royalty rate rather than a lump-sum payment; that is the payment to the author increases with the book's sales. For the publisher, the advantage of payment by royalty is that it gives the author an incentive to produce a high-quality output. In a government incentive contract, the cost-share parameter, α, plays the same role as a royalty rate: it gives the contractor appropriate incentives by making his payment depend on his performance. The prevalence in the private sector of payment schemes such as royalties and commissions suggests that the cost of administering contracts that relate payment to performance is not unduly high.[3]

7. THE GENERAL LINEAR CONTRACT

A way of expressing any government/firm contract is

(5) $\quad \tau = \alpha c + \beta b + \gamma.$

Here τ is the payment made by the government to the winning firm. This is composed of three terms. First, a proportion of the final cost is paid, and this proportion is called α. Second, a proportion β of the bid is paid. Finally, a fixed payment γ is also made; γ might be a given profit level.

Each of the contract forms in use in government/firm contracting is a special case of this linear contract. Thus the contract is fixed-price (equation 1) if $\alpha = 0$, $\beta = 1$, and $\gamma = 0$. The contract is an incentive contract (equation 4) if $0 < \alpha < 1$, $\beta = 1 - \alpha$, and $\gamma = 0$. The contract is a cost-plus contract if either $\alpha = 1$, $\beta = 0$, and $\gamma = 0$ (equation 2) or $\alpha = 1 + \theta$, $\beta = 0$, and $\gamma = 0$ (equation 3).

Provided the contract is not cost-plus (that is, provided $\alpha < 1$), the lowest-cost firm bids lowest and therefore bids reveal relative expected costs. For the general linear contract (equation 5), the requirement that the final payment to the firm be positively related to its bid requires both that $\alpha < 1$ and that $\beta > 0$.

---

3   There is a divergence here between theory and practice. In theory, the production costs upon which payment under an incentive contract is based are opportunity costs. However, opportunity costs can be observed only by the firm and not by the government. Hence the contract cannot workably be made contingent on the firm's opportunity cost. The imperfect but feasible solution is to make payment in the incentive contract depend on accounting costs. (This is imperfect because it unavoidably leaves the firm bearing the risk of unforeseen changes in opportunity costs.)

Indeed, as long as $\beta > 0$, the only parameter that matters is the cost-share parameter, α. That is, the government's expected payment will not be affected by the values the government assigns to the bid parameter, β, and to the constant term γ.

This rather surprising result follows from the bidding competition. Competition in bidding will lead a firm to bid low because, if it does not, some other firm will obtain the contract. What is of interest to the firm is revenue; the form of the revenue—whether it is allocated for the firm's costs, its bid, or the constant term—is immaterial. The values assigned to β and γ determine the form of the revenue, but not the amount of the revenue, which is determined by the competition for the contract. Thus an increase in γ will cause all the potential contractors to lower their bids by just the amount necessary (namely γ/β) to ensure that the government's expected payment to the successful firm is unchanged. The government's choice of β and γ affects the nominal size of the bids, but not (provided $\beta > 0$) the total cost of the project to the government. What this analysis suggests is that cost overruns are irrelevant. Indeed as long as $\beta > 0$, the only parameter that matters is the cost-share parameter, α. In other words, provided the bid parameter, β, is positive, the government's expected payment will not be affected by the values the government assigns to β and to the constant term γ.

This point requires some simplification. What is of interest to a firm is the revenue that it stands to obtain if it wins the contract. The form of the revenue—whether it is allocated for the winning firm's costs, its bid on the constant term—is immaterial. The amount of the revenue is determined by the bidding competition—that is, the size of the profit margin implicit in a firm's bid is determined by how close the next-lowest-cost firm's costs are to its own costs. The value of the cost-share parameter, α, determines the intensity of the bidding competition and hence the amount of revenue that will accrue to the winning firm. But the values of the bid parameter, β, and the constant term γ merely determine the form that the revenue will take. Thus an increase in γ will cause all the potential contractors to lower their bids by just the amount necessary (namely γ/β) to ensure that the winning firm's revenue—and thus the government's expected payment—will be unchanged. The amount of revenue that the winning firm loses by reducing its bid is made up in payments for its cost overruns. The government's choice of β and γ affects the nominal size of the bids, but not (provided $\beta > 0$) the total cost of the project to the government.

What this analysis suggests is that concern about cost overruns is unwarranted. A cost overrun is not in itself of any significance. What matters is the total cost of the project to the government, and the only thing the government can do to minimize its total cost is to choose the optimal value of the cost-share parameter, α. Again, the government can set the constant term γ and the target profit rate β in equation 5 arbitrarily, so long as β is strictly positive.

8. THE IRRELEVANCE OF COST OVERRUNS

Concern is often expressed about cost overruns in government contracts. Our theoretical analysis shows that such concern is unwarranted. A cost overrun is not in itself of any significance; what matters is the total cost of the project to the government. Even if a contract has been constructed to minimize the government's expected payment, there may on average be a cost overrun.

To see this, recall that the only thing the government must do to minimize its expected payment is to choose the optimal cost-share parameter. In equation 5, the government can set the constant term γ and the target profit rate β arbitrarily, so long as β is strictly positive. The higher the government sets γ and β, the greater is the value of winning the contract and therefore the lower the bids will be. The lower the bids are, the more likely it is that the realized cost will exceed the selected firm's bid; that is, there will be a cost overrun. What the government loses through the cost overrun exactly matches what it gains through the lower bid. Hence, provided the cost-share parameter is optimal, cost overruns are inconsequential. Persistent or large cost overruns are not in themselves evidence of mismanagement by the government.

However, cost overruns are only inconsequential if the contract is optimally designed. Cost overruns are a cause for concern if they are symptoms of poorly designed or poorly administered contracts. In particular, a cost overrun under a cost-plus contract is symptomatic of the cost-plus contract's failings. With a cost-plus contract, as we said earlier, a firm's bid bears no relationship to the firm's expected cost. The firm knows that its costs, however high they turn out to be, will be covered by the government, so it deliberately underbids in order to win the contract. Thus one would expect cost overruns to be the norm with cost-plus contracts—as in fact they are.

A fixed-price contract or an incentive contract will become, in effect, an ad hoc cost-plus contract if the government is unduly willing to change the terms of the contract after the contract has been awarded. If the bidding firm believes it will be able to persuade the government to raise the agreed-upon price during the course of the project, then it will deliberately underbid. Bids will not reveal relative expected costs; the lowest-cost firm will not necessarily win the contract. In such cases, since bids are set below expected costs, cost overruns are symptoms of government mismanagement.

9. OVERCHARGING BY CONTRACTORS

We have discussed cost padding by the contractor as one of the activities the government might seek to influence through its choice of the cost-share parameter, α. However, as our analysis of the general linear contract shows, there is one kind of cost padding that need be of no concern to the government, because it does not increase the cost of the project to the government.

A common source of public concern about government contracting is newspaper reports about contractors who overcharge the government for inputs used—thus a contractor might assign a cost of $500 to a wrench that actually cost $1.

Suppose that, before the contract is awarded, all bidders know they will be permitted to charge the government $500 for a wrench that will cost them $1 to acquire. This circumstance will, in effect, add $499 to the profit that accrues to the successful bidder. But if all bidders know this in advance, competition will drive down the bids by exactly this amount. The amount the contractor gains by his overcharging is cancelled out by the amount he had to lower his bid in order to win the contract. In the general linear contract (equation 5), the ability to overcharge is like the constant term γ, which has no effect on the government's ultimate payment.

This argument relies on a number of assumptions that may or may not be met in an actual contracting situation. First, all of the potential contractors must have similar estimates of how much they will be able to overcharge if they win the contract. Second, since the argument is based on the effects of competition in bidding, the contract must be put up for competitive tender and not awarded on a sole source basis. Finally, the contract must not be a cost-plus contract, since the beneficial effects of bidding competition are lost if the contract is cost-plus.

10. INCENTIVES AND QUALITY

The theoretical model just described assumes that the contractor can alter costs at his discretion. If the contractor is not given appropriate incentives, he may either fail to exert effort to keep costs low or fraudulently charge the government for costs not actually incurred. The converse of charging the government for costs not actually incurred is claiming that the work is of a higher quality than it really is. In some circumstances, the contractor may face a temptation to do work of a quality inferior to that specified in the contract.

Quality incentives and cost incentives work in opposite directions. Recall that the incentives for cost reduction are strongest under a fixed-price contract and weakest under a cost-plus contract. Incentives for doing high-quality work, in contrast, strengthen as the cost-share parameter increases: they are strongest under a cost-plus contract and weakest under a fixed-price contract. Under a fixed-price contract, each dollar saved by reducing production costs increases the contractor's profit by a dollar. Thus the contractor may try to lower production costs by skimping on quality. Under an incentive contract with cost-share parameter α, the contractor keeps only a fraction $(1 - \alpha)$ of any cost reduction. As α increases towards 1, therefore, the contractor gains less from reducing costs; his incentives for cheating on quality decline correspondingly. At the extreme of a cost-plus contract ($\alpha = 1$), the contractor's profit is independent of his production costs and he has no reason not to meet the project's specifications in full.[4]

11. AUDITING POLICY

Our analysis assumed that the government's objective is to obtain work of adequate quality from the contractor at the lowest possible price. This assumption ignores the fact that the government also faces the costs of administering the contract. Such costs can be neglected only if they are small relative to the value of the contract, which they may very well be if the contract is worth hundreds of thousands of dollars or more.

Consideration of administration costs can affect the choice of optimal contract. Because payment under incentive contracts and cost-plus contracts depends on the costs incurred by the contractor, some auditing of contractors' claims may be required to ensure that the claimed costs have actually been incurred. While fixed-price contracts do not require auditing, since payment does not vary with costs, they are not costless to administer: it is necessary to check that the contractor's work is up to the required standard. As we have just seen, the contractor's temptation to save costs by skimping on quality is stronger under a fixed-price contract than under any other form of contract. Thus the costs to the government of checking the quality of workmanship will tend to be higher under fixed-price contracts than under incentive contracts or cost-plus contracts.

Under cost-plus contracts, it is common government practice to supervise the contractor's work directly. In effect, this means that there is 100 per cent auditing: every cost claim of the contractor is checked by the government. It is likely that a more cost-effective strategy would be for the government to audit only some cost claims (or parts of some) and let others go unaudited. Clearly, this practice would reduce administrative costs. If the probability that any one claim will be audited is high enough and the punishment for fraud (either a fine or the loss of the chance to win future government contracts) is severe enough, contractors will not usually attempt to defraud the government. Auditing could be done at random; or there could be some audit cut-off policy, under which cost claims that appeared to be unusually high would be audited. There is a useful analogy here with the policies of the taxation authorities: the existence of some probability of being audited is enough to deter most people from filing false income tax statements.[5]

Under incentive contracts, the extent to which cost claims need be audited

---

4   Quality choice by the contractor is not included in our theoretical model. It could be incorporated as negative cost padding, a step that would involve some slight notational complication but no essential changes in the results. Adding the quality decision would slightly increase the optimal cost-share parameter α^*.

5   For a theoretical analysis of optimal auditing policies, see Reinganum and Wilde (1984). Bailey et al. (1981a, b, c; 1982a, b, c) consider auditing from an internal control viewpoint. For a discussion of the practical aspects of auditing in government contracting, see Riemer (1968: 841-50).

for auditing to be effective depends on the value the government assigns to the cost-share parameter, α. If the optimal contract is near the fixed-price end of the spectrum (e.g., $\alpha = 0.1$), the contractor will have little incentive to inflate his costs. A very small probability of detection will be enough to deter most fraud, and thus the government's auditing costs will be low. As α increases, however, the contractor's temptation to inflate costs becomes stronger. If fraud is to be deterred, the probability of detection must rise. The government must do more auditing. Thus the government's administrative costs increase as α increases.

To see how random auditing might be applied to cost-plus contracts, consider the expected return to the firm for overcharging for a good or service. Suppose the firm charges \$110 for a \$10 hammer, for a net gain of \$100, and let p be the probability that this overcharging is detected. If the penalty for overcharging is triple damages, then the firm will lose \$300 when it is caught and gain \$100 when it is not caught. Consequently the firm's expected return on cheating is

$$p \cdot (-\$300) + (1 - p) \times \$100 = \$100 - p \cdot \$400.$$

If p exceeds 25 per cent, the firm can expect to lose from overcharging; 25 per cent is the break-even point for triple damages, since

$$(0.25)(-\$300) + (0.75)(\$100) = \$0.$$

Therefore catching 25 per cent of these illicit earnings should be enough to deter all cases of overcharging. Overcharging ceases to pay with a random auditing policy of 25 per cent.

Note that any increase in the penalty for overcharging lowers the break-even probability. For example, quadruple damages lower the probability to 20 per cent, since

$$(0.2)(-\$400) + (0.8)(\$100) = \$0.$$

Under an incentive contract, an increase in cost of \$100 produces $\alpha \cdot \$100$ in revenue. Thus, if the penalty for overcharging is triple damages, the firm's expected earnings are

$$p \cdot (-\$300) + \alpha(1 - p)\$100 = \alpha \cdot \$100 - p(\$300 + \alpha \cdot \$100).$$

The break-even point occurs when

$$p = \alpha/(3 + \alpha).$$

For example, if α is 10 per cent, the proportion of claims that must be audited to deter overcharging is 3.2 per cent. Thus for low values of the incentive parameter, α, the corresponding auditing costs are also low. Consequently, auditing costs are not an objection to the use of incentive contracts.

It is important to stress that the purpose of auditing, as a policy tool, is not so much to detect illegal behaviour as it is to deter this behaviour. As we have seen, auditing of 25 per cent of claims is sufficient to deter overcharging in all cases, given triple damages, and in fact, 25 per cent is probably a vast overestimate of the necessary amount of auditing. Damages are only part of the penalty for overcharging. The firm also suffers a loss of reputation and therefore a loss of future income, since both the government and other private firms will tend to avoid dealing with the firm. Because reputation effects last a long time, the loss of future income may outweigh the direct monetary cost of damages. Even if the value of the lost business is only six times the amount overcharged, the break-even probability drops to 10 per cent under a cost-plus contract. Since the potential gains from overcharging are usually very small relative to future profits, 10 per cent is probably still an overestimate of the amount of auditing necessary to deter cost padding. Indeed, auditing only 3 per cent of personal income tax returns appears to effectively deter tax evasion. (Of course, the possible penalties for tax evasion include incarceration, which has a large deterrent effect.)

Risk aversion also reduces the probability of auditing necessary to deter cost padding. Under a strategy of random audits, cost padding is inherently risky. Risk-averse firms must earn higher expected returns to justify the activity. For example, if it takes an expected return of $20 to justify $100 of cost padding, the break-even probability is determined by

$$p \cdot (-\$300) + (1 - p)(\$100) = \$20,$$

which yields a p of 20 per cent instead of 25 per cent. In addition, cost padding involves the worst kind of risk, since the potential losses are large relative to the potential gains.

We can conclude from these examples that, even in the case of cost-plus contracts, an auditing frequency of 10 per cent is probably sufficient. For incentive contracts, the necessary auditing frequencies are, of course, even smaller. If we assume a risk premium of 20 per cent and assume arbitrarily that the cost of being detected is seven times the amount of the cost padding (three times for triple damages plus four times for reputational effects), then, as a rule of thumb, frequencies given by

$$p = 0.8\alpha/(7 + \alpha)$$

will effectively deter cost padding.

It must be stressed that randomness is crucial to the effectiveness of the auditing policy discussed here. Suppose, for example, that the taxation authority does not audit anyone with deductions of less than 20 per cent of declared income. Then anyone with legitimate deductions of, say, 10 per cent of declared income can claim fake deductions equal to 9 per cent of his income and be safe from an audit. Thus to exclude a group from auditing—that is, to follow a non-random policy—is to invite cost padding.

Nevertheless, sometimes different groups should be audited with different frequencies. In general, the larger are the rewards of illicit behaviour, the higher is the probability of auditing necessary to deter the behaviour. Thus, the easier it is to pad costs, the higher is the frequency of auditing necessary to deter cost padding. Within a group, however, the auditing policy should be random.

The level of auditing necessary to deter cost padding completely is not the same as the level necessary to minimize the cost of contracting to the government. Suppose an auditing frequency of 20 per cent deters cost padding completely. Then a level of 19.99 per cent will deter virtually all cost padding. A movement from 19.99 per cent to 20 per cent will not appreciably increase the deterrent effect, and it will reduce the revenue raised by auditing. (One makes money from auditing only if one catches cheaters. If one completely deters cheating, one raises no revenue in the process.) Moreover, there is a positive cost associated with auditing. In short, the government loses money from complete deterrence. If the government's objective is to obtain contracted services at the lowest possible cost, it will not completely deter cost padding. Indeed, this consideration could reduce the optimal auditing frequency by as much as half.

To summarize: An auditing frequency between 5 per cent and 25 per cent is probably sufficient to deter cost padding under a cost-plus contract. Incentive contracts require less auditing; indeed, the necessary frequency decreases smoothly with the cost-share parameter, α. Thus the cost of auditing is not an objection to employing incentive contracts. High penalties for either fraud or risk aversion lower the necessary frequency. Finally, the optimal amount of auditing depends on the government's objective. If the government's goal is to minimize its costs, it will perform fewer audits than it would perform if its goal were a complete elimination of cost padding.

The effect of taking contract administration costs into consideration is to reduce the optimal cost-share parameter, α^*. If the previous analysis, ignoring administration costs, indicated a very low value for the α^*—say 0.05—then adding administration costs might reduce α^* to zero, making the fixed-price contract optimal.

12. CONTINGENT CONTRACTS AND CHANGES IN PAYMENT

Our analysis has assumed that the firm knows more about its own costs than the government knows, since the firm is in a better position to observe the vagaries of a project that cause production costs to fluctuate. In some circumstances, however, the government's knowledge of costs may equal the firm's knowledge.

The government might obtain its knowledge by assigning an observer to the work site, for example.

If the government's information is equal to the firm's, the problems of moral hazard and cost padding disappear—an advantage that may more than offset the cost to the government of keeping itself informed. Moreover, given equal information on both sides, a contract can be written that makes payment contingent upon relevant events. For example, the payment for construction of a road can be made contingent on the hardness of the soil. Such a contract further reduces the government's payment, since it reduces the firm's uncertainty about its profits: the contractor does not bear the risk of unpredictable extra costs because his payment varies directly with the underlying causes of the cost increases.

A contingent contract is clearly superior to the optimal contract as we defined it earlier. However, a contingent contract is feasible only if both parties have equal access to information about the relevant contingencies; payment cannot workably be made contingent upon an event that one party cannot observe.[6] While it would be too costly, though not in principle impossible, to write a contract that specified in advance the amount of payment in every possible eventuality, even contracts that take just one contingency into account can bring substantial benefits to both parties. For example, the problem of cost increases that result from inflation can be addressed by allowing the payment to increase in accordance with some official price index. Obviously, access to such an index is available to both the government and the firm. Making payment contingent upon the inflation removes some of the risk that the firm would otherwise be required to bear if the contract were anything but cost-plus. Thus, to the extent that firms are risk averse, making payment contingent upon inflation reduces the government's expected payment.

Contingent contracts can also be used to advantage when there are significant differences between accounting costs and opportunity costs. Generally, since accounting cost is observed, it is desirable to adjust the contract for changes in opportunity costs. For example, the opportunity cost to a firm of building a road depends on its other opportunities, which in turn depend on the general demand for road construction. Thus it may be useful to partially insure the firm against changes in its opportunities by making payment contingent on some measure of industry demand, such as the unemployment rate among construction firms. Use of such a measure will insure the firm against swings in demand in precisely the same way as the use of some measure of inflation will insure it against swings in inflation.[7]

For both purposes, in fact, the best measure may be an industry-specific index of inflation, when one is available. The use of an industry-specific measure will insure the firm against cost inflation more accurately than a general

6   On contingent contracts, see Debreu (1959), Hurwicz (1972), Shavell (1984), and Macaulay (1963).
7   We are grateful to Dr Jack Levenstein for this observation.

measure such as the Consumer Price Index. Since high opportunity costs generally cause the prices of labour and materials to rise, the same measure may also be used to insure the firm against major swings in its opportunity cost. In any specific application, it will be necessary to employ a great deal of information about the firm's opportunities. It will generally be possible, however, to save some government money by attempting to specify the types of cost variation facing the firm and making payment contingent on these.

It is sometimes necessary to change the terms of a contract after it has been written, perhaps because of an unpredictable change in the government's needs or because the project's original specifications are discovered to be infeasible. Because an incentive contract involves more parameters than a fixed-price contract, it may be somewhat more difficult to renegotiate. Renegotiation need not, however, be overwhelmingly difficult or costly. Provided the required changes are not large relative to the overall size of the project, an appropriate solution is simply to leave the cost-share parameter, α, at its original level and renegotiate the target (or bid) cost in the same way as the price would be renegotiated if the contract were fixed-price.[8]

13. MACROECONOMIC IMPLICATIONS

Some brief comments are in order on the interaction between government contracting and the overall state of the economy. There are two reasons why governments are likely to award more contracts during a recession than they award when the economy is booming.

First, there is the familiar Keynesian stabilization argument. To the extent that fiscal policy is effective, an increase in government expenditure on construction and other activities tends to counteract the ill-effects of a slump.

Second, the government can have work done at a lower cost to itself during a recession. Recall that the firms' costs may be interpreted as opportunity costs: they include profits forgone from alternative activities. In boom times, firms have highly profitable alternative activities and so their opportunity costs of doing government work are high; in a recession, firms face a low demand for their services and so their opportunity costs are low. Since firms bid lower the lower are their (opportunity) costs, firms will tend to bid low during a recession; the government's payments will be correspondingly low.

14. SUMMARY

The costs of any particular project are rarely perfectly predictable. The ultimate

---

8   For a detailed discussion of how to administer changes in incentive contracts, see Riemer (1968: 396-411, 617-43).

cost of building a road may be higher than the initial estimate because of unforeseen geological problems. The cost of building a nuclear power plant may increase because of the need to develop new technologies there may be unforeseen increases in labour or interest costs. A fixed-price contract requires the contractor to bear all of the risks of unpredictable cost increases. In order to induce the firm to bear this risk, the government must offer it a high rate of return. Moreover, the fixed-price contract fails to stimulate competition in bidding. Thus, although the fixed-price contract does induce the firm to minimize production costs, it may still be expensive for the government.

Provided there is more than one bidder, the pure cost-plus contract cannot be optimal. Since the firm's actual costs are completely paid by the government, the firm's expected costs are irrelevant in determining its bid. Bids do not reveal relative expected costs. The government will, in all likelihood, choose a high-cost firm. Thus the cost-plus contract is never ideal from the government's point of view.

An incentive contract both gives the firm an incentive to minimize costs and divides the risk of unforeseen cost increases between the government and the firm. Under an incentive contract, the government pays the firm a fee plus some fraction of any excess of actual costs over projected costs. The firm is itself responsible for the remaining fraction of the cost overrun. The incentive contract, by combining features of the fixed-price contract and the cost-plus contract, mitigates the ill effects of both.

While there are conditions under which the fixed-price contract is the optimal contract, these conditions are often not met. Then the optimal contract form is an incentive contract: using an incentive contract rather than a fixed-price contract or a cost-plus contract will result in savings for the government.

The simplicity of using an incentive contract should be emphasized. Chapter 5 will demonstrate that a government agency can reduce the computation of an approximately optimal cost-share parameter for each contract to a routine procedure. The firm takes as given the cost-share parameter chosen by the government. For the firm, working under an incentive contract need be no more difficult than working under other payment schemes, such as commission or royalty schemes, that make payment vary with performance.

4

Competition in Bidding

Competition in bidding serves two purposes: it drives down bids and therefore lowers the price the government must pay for the project; and it reveals relative expected costs, since (according to the model described in Chapter 3) the lowest-cost firm bids lowest.

The analysis in Chapter 3 indicated that one of the crucial determinants of the optimal contract is the extent of bidding competition. If bidding competition is very strong and the firms are risk neutral, the optimal contract is a fixed-price contract. Weak competition in bidding will tend to make the optimal contract an incentive contract that is close to being a cost-plus contract. If an incentive contract is optimal, then the stronger is the bidding competition the smaller is the optimal cost-share parameter.

By the nature of the open tendering process, data on each firm's bid for any contract are public information. This chapter uses Ontario and other data to analyse empirically the extent of bidding competition for government contracts.

The results of this empirical exercise have relevance not only for policy but also for economic theory. The theoretical innovation of the model described in Chapter 3 is its addition of the agent-selection or tendering process to a principal/agent model whose properties have been thoroughly analysed in the economic-theory literature. The addition of the agent-selection process changes the standard principal/agent theory in important ways. This chapter's empirical analysis of the extent of bidding competition allows some assessment of the practical importance of these changes.

1. SOLE-SOURCE PROCUREMENT VERSUS COMPETITIVE PROCUREMENT

A study by the US Congress's Joint Economic Committee Department of Defense weapon-procurement practices provides a striking demonstration of the power of competition to lower the price paid by the government (see Yuspeh

TABLE 4.1
Reduction in unit price due to competition: examples from US Department of Defence Procurement

System	Sole source			Competitive			Unit-price reduction (per cent)
	Contractor	Date	Unit price (1970 dollars)	Contractor	Date	Unit price (1970 dollars)	
60-640 Electrical control	General Electric	1968	6,927	Lear Siegler	1969	3,030	56
AN/SQS-23208A Transducer	Dynamics Corp. of America	1967	75,884	Hazeltine	1967	40,249	47
Rockeye bomb	Honeywell	1970	2,309	1. Honeywell	1971	1,882	19
				2. Marquardt	1971	1,641	29
MK-48 Torpedo							
1. Warhead	Delco	1971	11,019	Goodyear Aerospace	1972	5,087	54
2. Exploder	Delco	1970	25,800	Goodyear Aerospace	1971	5,165	80
3. Electric assembly	Delco	1971	13,356	Goodyear Aerospace	1972	6,027	55
4. Test set	Delco	1970	69,525	Goodyear Aerospace	1971	14,717	79
Sandard Missile ER R1M 67A	General	1966	149,766	General Dynamics	1967	61,039	59
Standard Missile MR R1M 66A	General	1966	149,766	General Dynamics	1967	60,230	60
APX-72	Bendix	1970	2,766	Honeywell	1970	1,653	40
Hank Mtr Metal Brts	Aerojet General Corp.	1960-61	1,778	Intercontinental Mfg.	1964	891	50
Electronics series							
1. TD-352 Multiplexer	Raytheon	1968	10,269	Honeywell	1968	4,291	58
2. TD-204 Cable combiner	Raytheon	1968	3,755	Honeywell	1968	1,877	50
3. TD-660 Multiplexer	Raytheon	1969	5,949	Honeywell	1969	3,527	41
4. TD-202 Radio combiner	Raytheon	1968	3,366	Honeywell	1967	2,322	31
SPA-66 Radar indicator	Hazeltine	1963	10,462	Hazeltine	1970	8,800	16
Bullpup 12-B missile	Martin	1961	4,969	Martin	1961	3,725	25
Taltos missile	Bendix	1965	159,263	Bendix	1966	92,249	42
ARA-63 Rad. recdec set	AIL Co.	1969	7,849	ASC Systems Corp.	1972	2,822	63

SOURCE: Yuspeh (1976: 108-11)

1976). The study examined unit prices on major weapons systems that had been procured first on a sole-source basis and later by competitive bidding. The data are summarized in Table 4.1, which compares the lowest sole-source price with the highest competitive price, thus providing a lower-bound estimate of the savings attributable to competition. The switch from sole-source procurement to competitive procurement resulted in large savings, ranging from 16 per cent to 80 per cent with a mean of 51 per cent.[1]

The theoretical analysis in Chapter 3 indicated two reasons why the price is lower with competition: first, firms are forced by the presence of competitors to bid low in order to win the contract; second, the bidding for any contract open to competition, other than a cost-plus contract, reveals relative expected costs, whereas with a sole-source contract there is no guarantee that the lowest-cost firm has been selected. The data in Table 4.1 show the strength of this bidding-competition effect: on average, the presence of competition halved the price paid by the government.

For large construction contracts, the City of Chicago awards what it calls, with candour, 'no-bid contracts. 'As the name implies, these contracts are awarded on a sole-source basis. In September 1984 there was a protracted battle between the mayor and the city council in which each side tried to claim the authority to award the no-bid contracts (*Los Angeles Times*, 2 October 1984). Why Chicago's politicians would struggle for the power to control the no-bid contracts must be left to conjecture.

The foregoing data compared prices with and without bidding competition. A more subtle problem is to determine the effects of introducing more or less bidding competition. These effects must be identified before it is possible to address this question: how much bidding competition is enough bidding competition?

2. THE EXTENT OF BIDDING COMPETITION

The theoretical analysis established that the firms' bids are lower, and therefore the government's expected payment is lower as well, (a) the more bidders there are and (b) the smaller is the variance in the bids (which reflects the variance in the firms' expected costs).

How much bidding competition occurs in government tenders? Table 4.2 presents data for a sample of large construction contracts awarded by the Ontario Ministry of Government Services. The contracts are all fixed-price contracts. For the 21 contracts, the number of bidders ranged from 1 to 31; the average was 11.4. The third and fourth columns of Table 4.2 show, for each contract, the lowest bid and the highest bid.

We have used these data to estimate the properties of the distributions of

---

1   Other studies, using different samples of contracts, have estimated that the average cost difference between sole-source and competitively procured contracts is 25 per cent (Fox 1974: 256), 32 per cent (Fox 1974: 256), and 33 per cent (Gansler 1980: 298).

TABLE 4.2
Large construction contracts from Ontario Ministry of Government Services, 1982-83

Contract	Number of bidders	Lowest bid	Highest bid	Estimated minimum cost, c_l	Estimated maximum cost, c_k	Estimated savings from one extra bidder — In dollars	Estimated savings from one extra bidder — In per cent
1	8	260,175	335,290	263,703	374,076	2,453	0.94
2	8	2,429,000	2,647,000	2,574,963	2,895,290	7,118	0.29
3	18	312,093	407,923	333,688	447,092	597	0.19
4	12	545,900	578,000	586,635	628,020	455	0.08
5	31	56,940	84,242	61,963	92,056	57	0.10
6	12	2,709,555	3,420,000	2,851,174	3,767,120	10,065	0.37
7	15	1,255,000	1,526,000	1,338,820	1,670,656	2,440	0.19
8	11	503,000	676,759	521,054	750,416	2,941	0.58
9	5	198,800	312,200	155,537	368,162	10,125	5.09
10	3	26,900	34,500	18,605	41,405	2,280	8.48
11	1	210,000	210,000				
12	9	599,637	833,700	603,776	932,927	5,985	1.00
13	8	887,000	1,064,000	917,525	1,177,606	5,780	0.65
14	12	705,000	1,069,000	722,160	1,191,450	5,157	0.73
15	13	360,500	586,822	368,746	654,792	2,724	0.76
16	14	353,402	525,649	368,559	582,593	1,784	0.50
17	10	299,732	374,400	312,325	413,726	1,536	0.51
18	17	347,828	464,766	370,573	510,351	817	0.24
19	16	1,620,000	2,044,000	1,727,719	2,240,288	3,350	0.21
20	7	594,000	828,828	573,054	938,342	10,147	1.71
21	7	218,800	294,134	213,782	334,079	3,342	1.53

SOURCE: Computed from data supplied by the Ontario Ministry of Government Services

TABLE 4.3
Sample of construction and maintenance contracts—Ontario Ministry of Transporation and Communications, 1984

Contract	Number of bidders	Lowest bid	Highest bid	Estimated minimum cost c_l	Estimated maximum cost c_u	Estimated savings from one extra bidder	
						In dollars	In per cent
1	2	674,223	688,442	674,320	759,634	14,219	2.11
2	4	1,085,020	1,385,220	938,604	1,605,715	44,474	4.10
3	4	48,345	58,852	44,061	67,410	1,557	3.22
4	1	134,046	134,046				
5	1	105,939	105,939				
6	2	152,741	158,097	144,570	176,706	5,356	3.51
7	2	213,142	213,614	228,612	231,444	472	0.22
8	7	4,142,150	5,202,600	4,165,916	5,185,505	45,822	1.11
9	3	448,520	539,469	359,524	632,371	27285	6.08
10	3	1,061,000	1,094,050	1,101,472	1,200,622	9,915	0.93
11	5	522,524	694,054	475,069	796,688	15,315	2.93
12	4	108,596	134,706	97,015	155,037	3,868	3.56
13	4	34,800	62,200	16,228	77,117	4,059	11.66
14	4	1,094,750	1,391,880	951,520	1,611,809	44,019	4.02
15	4	355,211	627,802	171,178	776,936	40,384	11.37
16	5	515,408	648,013	487,759	736,394	11,840	2.30
17	7	440,642	623,777	422,474	707,351	7,913	1.80
18	5	1,658,00	1,768,700	1,735,427	1,941,86	9,830	0.59
19	4	93,571	123,736	77,606	144,639	4,469	4.78
20	4	55,800	64,800	53,297	73,297	1,333	2.39
21	3	194,090	163,460	114,209	322,319	20,811	10.72
22	1	158,160	158,160				
23	3	921	945,695	961,772	1,035,692	7,392	0.80

SOURCE: Computed from data supplied by the Ontario Ministry of Transportation and Communications (1984)

TABLE 4.4
Sample of contracts from the Ontario Ministry of Natural Resources, 1983-84

Contract	Number of bidders	Lowest bid	Highest bid	Estimated minimum cost, c_ℓ	Estimated maximum cost, c_u	Estimated savings from one extra bidder	
						In dollars	In per cent
1	4	162,450	248,805	180,197	300,097	12,793	7.88
2	3	364,693	662,438	-60,413	886,822	94,724	27.32
2 *	4	329,005	662,438	95,342	836,305	63,149	19.19
3	4	228,760	249,158	231,383	276,708	3,022	1.32
4	3	131,579	146,040	122,315	165,698	4,338	3.30
5	8	117,400	420,00	56,151	500,788	9,881	8.42
6	5	145,742	272,672	91,092	329,086	11,333	7.78
7	3	398,400	437,680	376,560	494,400	11,784	2.96
8	10	1,713,000	3,351,146	1,594,992	3,819,635	33,707	1.97
9	10	829,700	1,397,570	807,918	1,579,099	11,685	1.41
10	8	173,540	376,800	104,075	438,743	6,637	3.82
11	7	121,780	190,349	111,475	218,137	2,963	2.43
12	5	200,700	264,424	183,604	303,086	5,690	2.83
13	4	160,820	231,770	118,463	276,130	10,511	6.54
14	9	25,276	60,444	20,642	70,097	899	3.56
15	8	38,000	79,392	31,401	92,222	1,352	3.56
16	8	31,500	75,650	23,729	88,602	1,442	4.58
17	6	17,500	34,860	12,275	41,440	1,042	5.95
18	8	35,238	59,700	32,374	68,318	799	2.27
19	9	37,756	73,199	34,082	83,924	906	2.40
20	10	242,201	358,610	243,583	401,670	2,395	0.99

SOURCE: Data supplied by the Ontario Ministry of Natural Resources
NOTE: The lowest bidder in contract 2 was disqualified. Line 2 calculates the estimates ignoring this bidder; line 2* includes him. Because the disqualified bidder evidently had an extreme effect on the winner's bid, line 2* is probably more appropriate in understanding this contract.

the firms' costs. In particular, we have estimated the highest and lowest expected costs a firm could possibly have for each project. The fifth and sixth columns of Table 4.2 report the estimated highest and lowest possible costs for each of the 21 projects.

Estimates of the range of possible costs can, in turn, be used to obtain estimates of the force of the bidding-competition effect. The extent of bidding competition depends on both the number of firms submitting bids and the dispersion of the firms' expected costs: the more firms there are bidding and the closer are their expected costs, the greater is the bidding competition. The reason for this is as follows. What constrains the lowest-cost firm in deciding how high to bid is the extent to which production cost of the second-lowest-cost firm is higher than its own production cost. If the lowest-cost firm bids any amount lower than the second-lowest-cost firm's production cost, it will certainly win the contract. The firm does not know its rivals' costs; indeed, it does not even know whether or not it is the lowest-costbidder. But it can predict on average how much above its own production cost it can bid and not run too great a risk of losing the contract. The greater is the number of bidders, the smaller on average is the difference between the lowest cost and the second-lowest-cost; hence the smaller is the profit margin that the lowest-cost firm can afford to build into its bid. Similarly, the smaller on average is the difference between lowest-cost and second-lowest cost, the smaller is the dispersion among the different firms' production costs; hence the lower are the firms' bids.

Suppose one additional firm had entered the bidding. By how much would the extra competition have driven down the price paid by the government? This question can be answered by using the model in Chapter 3. The last two columns of Table 4.2 present estimates for each contract of the government's expected savings, both in dollars and as a percentage of actual cost, if one extra firm had submitted a bid.

Table 4.3 presents data from a sample of fixed-price contracts for construction or maintenance work awarded by the Ontario Ministry of Transportation and Communications. The data are categorized in the same way as the data in Table 4.2. Notice that the number of bidders for these contracts is in most cases smaller than the number of bidders for Ministry of Government Services contracts.[2] For the 23 contracts, the number of bidders ranged from 1 to 7, with an average of 3.6. Table 4.4 provides analogous data from the Ministry of Natural Resources: in this sample, the number of bidders was between 3 and 10, with an average of 6.6.

3. CHANGES IN BIDDING COMPETITION

How much difference to the price paid by the government would be made by

---

2　As contract 11 in Table 4.2 and contracts 4, 5, and 22 in Table 4.3 show, the computation technique breaks down when there is only one bidder.

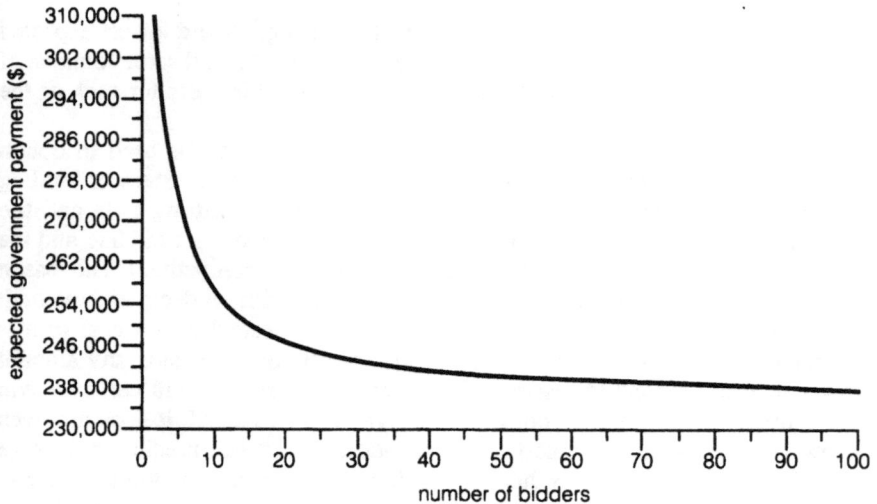

Figure 4.1
Simulation of the relationship between the government's expected payment and the number of bidders
SOURCE: Data from contract 1 of Table 4.2

changing the number of bidders? A partial answer to this question was given by Tables 4.2, 4.3, and 4.4, which reported estimates of the effects of having one extra bidder.

Consider any one contract from Table 4.2; the first contract serves as well as any other. Eight firms competed for that contract. Figure 4.1 plots estimates of what the lowest bid would have been on the average had there instead been anywhere between 2 and 100 bidders for that particular contract.[3]

Notice that Figure 4.1 shows a diminishing-returns effect. Increasing the number of bidders does reduce the price paid by the government, but this effect diminishes as more bidders are added. By the time the number of bidders reaches 20, the gains from adding further bidders have almost been exhausted.

Figures 4.2 and 4.3 are similar to Figure 4.1, but are based on the fifth contract from Table 4.2 and the twenty-first contract from Table 4.3. (These contracts were selected arbitrarily.)

The other determinant of bidding competition, as important as the number of bidders, is the extent of differences among the bidders' expected costs. The more widely the expected costs are dispersed, the less pressure there is on firms to bid low.

3 Gaver and Zimmermann (1977), in a study of bidding for contracts for the construction of San Francisco's BART subway system, and Gilley and Karels (1981), in a study of bidding for mineral rights to government owned land, found that the effect of the number of bidders on the size of bids was statistically significant.

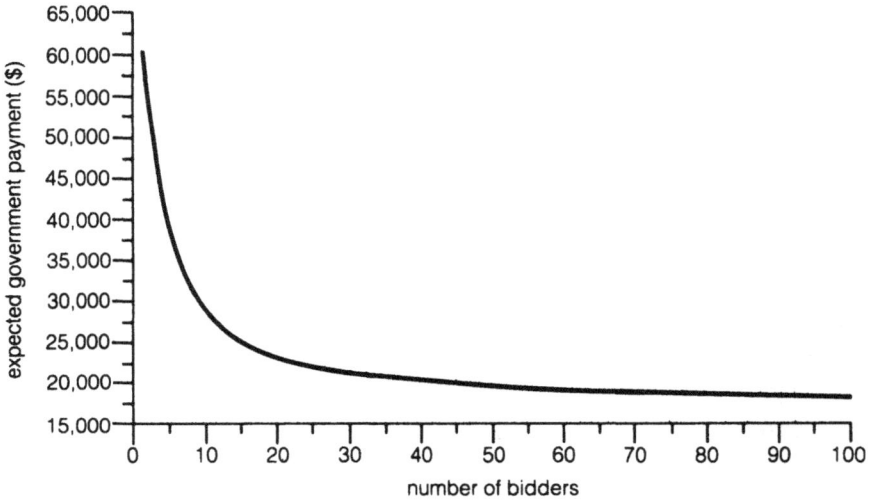

Figure 4.2
Simulation of the relationship between the government's expected payment and the number of bidders
SOURCE: Data from contract 16 of Table 4.4

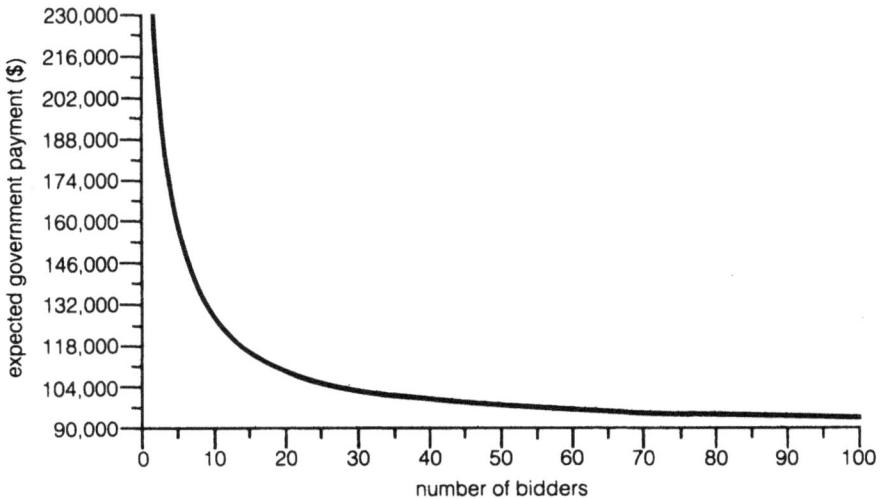

Figure 4.3
Simulation of the relationship between the government's expected payment and the number of bidders
SOURCE: Data from contract 21 of Table 4.3

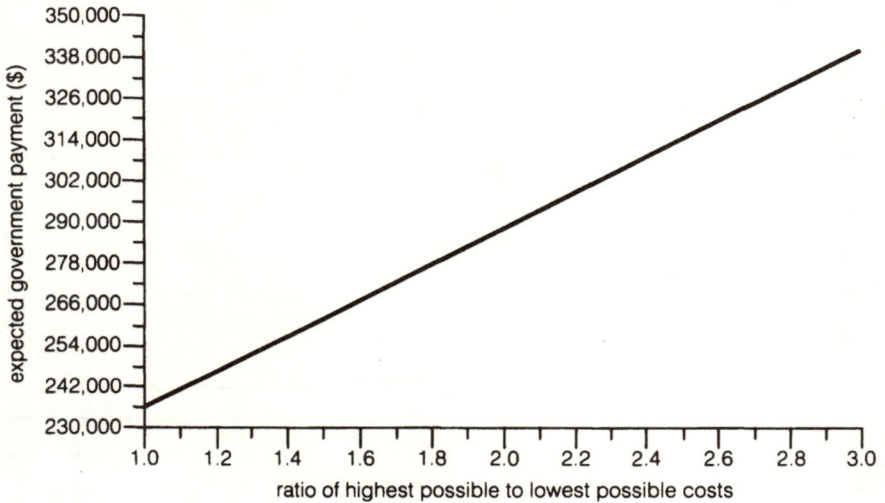

Figure 4.4
Simulation of the relationship between the government's expected payment and
the spread of bidders' expected costs
SOURCE: Same as Figure 4.1

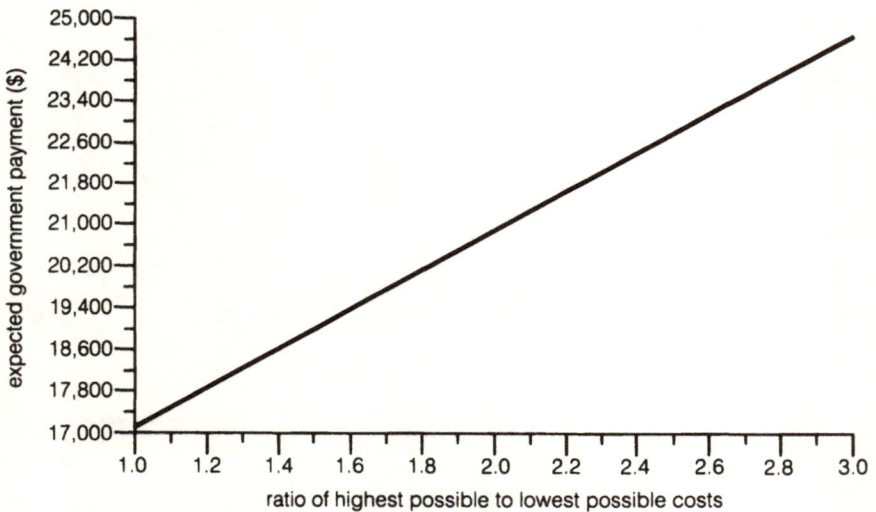

Figure 4.5
Simulation of the relationship between the government's expected payment and
the spread of bidders' expected costs
SOURCE: Same as Figure 4.2

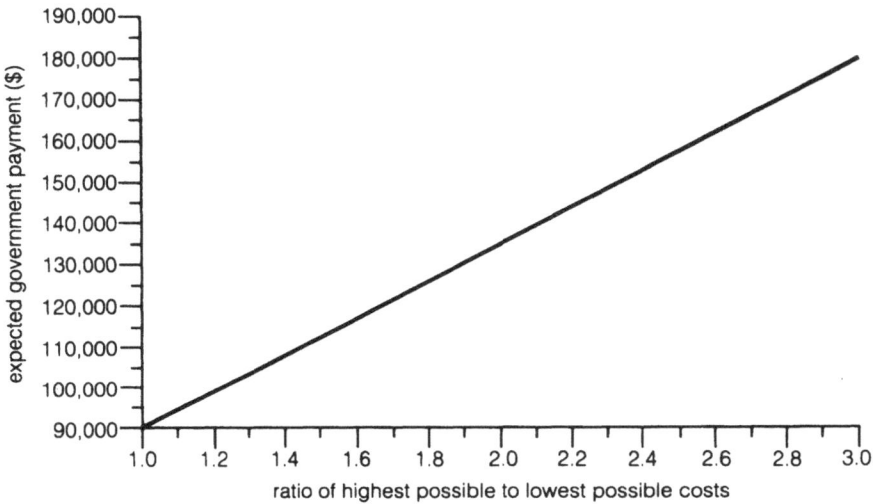

Figure 4.6
Simulation of the relationship between the government's expected payment and the spread of bidders' expected costs
SOURCE: Same as Figure 4.3

Figures 4.4, 4.5, and 4.6 (based on the same three contracts as Figures 4.1, 4.2, and 4.3, respectively) simulate the effects of varying the dispersion of firms' expected costs while holding constant the number of bidders. The lowest possible expected cost is held constant, and the highest expected cost is varied. As the highest expected cost approaches the lowest expected cost, the government's expected payment falls considerably.

4. POLICIES TO INCREASE BIDDING COMPETITION

Most of the methods for increasing bidding competition suggested in this section are not especially novel; they are already often used by government officials responsible for contracting. What is original to the present study is the technique it offers for estimating the gains from increasing bidding competition.

One way in which a government can increase the number of firms competing for contracts is by dividing a given project into several separate subprojects, if such a division is possible. Small projects are likely to attract more bidders than large projects, since firms capable of undertaking small projects might lack the resources to undertake large ones. The increased bidding competition for the subprojects will lower the price paid by the government for the total project.

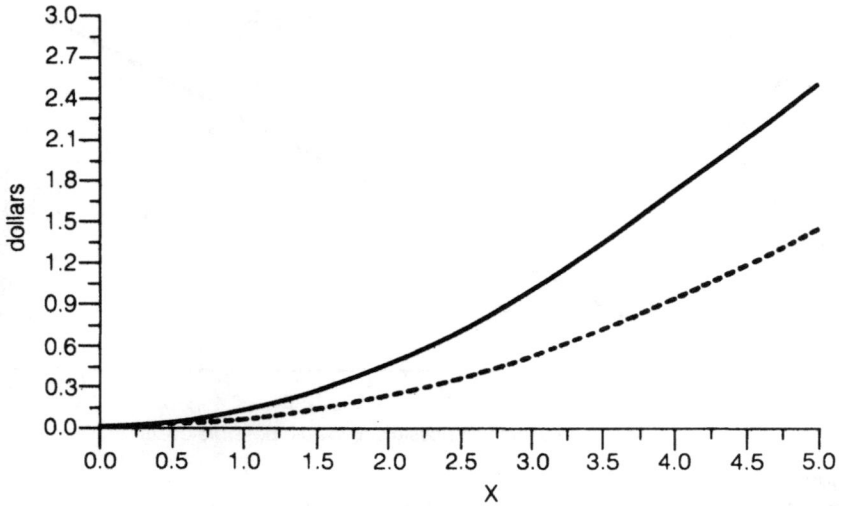

Figure 4.7
The dollar cost of a gamble with ±X outcomes, each with equal probability

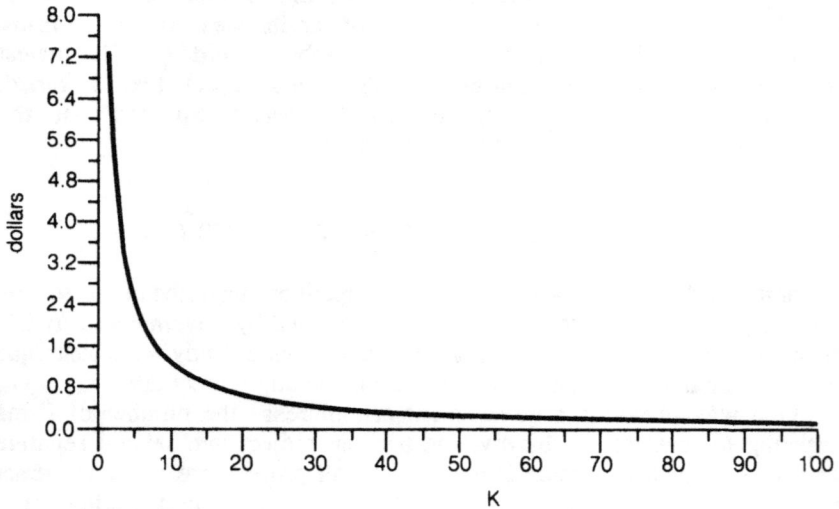

Figure 4.8
Total cost due to risk when the project is divided into K subprojects

There may also be gains to dividing up a project on the grounds of risk. Consider a project that consists of two risky subprojects. The first subproject has a cost of either $\mu + x$ or $\mu - x$, each with equal probability. The second subproject is analogous: its cost too is $\mu \pm x$. If the firm were risk neutral, it would do each subproject for the cost μ. Because many firms are not risk neutral, they will take the risk only if some extra payment, called a risk premium, is provided. Now suppose the costs are correlated: when the first subproject has high cost (that is, $\mu + x$), so does the second, and when the first subproject has low cost ($\mu - x$), so does the second. For a numerical example, consider a tree-planting project in northern Ontario. For simplicity suppose that either it rains and the cost is $1.25 per tree or it does not rain and the cost is $0.75 per tree ($\mu = \$1.00$, $x = \$0.25$), and that both of these outcomes are equally likely.

If there are two tracts of land to be planted 10,000 trees each, the cost on each tract will either be $7,500 or $12,500, with equal probability. If the tracts are adjacent, then the costs will be correlated, for if it rains on one, it rains on the other.

If a single firm does both jobs, its total cost will be either $15,000 (no rain) or $25,000 (rain). The opportunity cost of the project might be $22,500, which represents the average cost of $20,000 ($15,000 x 1/2 + $25,000 x 1/2) plus a risk premium of $2,500, to pay for the risk. If the job is given to two firms, each firm might be willing to do its share for $11,000, for a total cost of $22,000. This figure represents a saving of $500 through subdividing correlated risks.

There are always some savings from spreading out correlated risks. However, the bigger is the risk, the bigger is the saving. Consider again the example of the gamble in which an individual either gains or loses an amount x, each with equal probability (cf. Chapter 2). Figure 4.7 graphs the total cost of a risk of $\pm x$ against x with an unbroken line: doubling the risk more than doubles the cost of the risk. The broken line graphs total cost when the project is divided in half: dividing the job reduces the total cost of the risk.

Finally, Figure 4.8 graphs the total cost of the risk when a project is divided into n equally risky, correlated subprojects, for n ranging from 1 to 100. The gains from risk spreading diminish as n grows because the costs of dividing the project among several firms (including increased administrative costs and duplication of equipment and personnel) increase with the number of firms. The optimal subdivision of a large project is a task for which the knowledge of the government administrator is crucial, since so much depends on the particulars of the contract and the resources of the potential contractors. As a matter of fact, the Ontario Ministry of Natural Resources does divide the planting of trees in northern Ontario into tracts, each tendered separately.

Some possible disadvantages to breaking up projects must be weighed against the gains from risk spreading and increased bidding competition. First, economies of scale may be lost: the total production cost for the subprojects may be higher than the production cost of completing the project as a unit. Second, as we have already noted, breaking up the project may increase administrative costs. There may be difficulties in coordinating the work of different contractors, or delays may arise because one firm's subproject depends on the completion of another firm's subproject. Obviously the gains and losses associated with subdivision must be evaluated on a project-by-project basis.

There are other ways in which a government can increase bidding competition. It can publicize upcoming contract awards widely enough to ensure that all capable firms learn of the opportunity to bid. It can set a time limit for the submission of bids long enough to enable all interested firms to draw up their bids. It can take care to define a project's technical specifications in terms broad enough to ensure that no firm will be excluded from the bidding because its equipment, though capable of doing the work, is not exactly the type called for in the specifications.

By publicizing new and less costly technologies, a government may be able to reduce its expected payments in two ways. First, since the government's payment is equal to the firm's expected cost plus its profit, the availability of less costly technologies will tend to reduce payments. Second, disseminating information about technologies may reduce the dispersion among the different firms' expected costs. If the difference between the highest possible cost and the lowest possible cost is lessened, then, as we have already shown, the amount of bidding competition increases. Firms' profits will be driven down, and the government's payments will be reduced accordingly.

The Ontario government's Office of Procurement Policy is to be commended for facilitating the dissemination of information about opportunities for firms to bid. While it is too early to verify the office's success in lowering the government's contracting costs, this success can be presumed to follow from the increased bidding competition that the office stimulates by serving as a clearing-house for contracting information. The office might bring further benefits if it acted as a source of technical information as well, although the administrative costs of such an undertaking might outweigh the benefits.

Finally, the government should, if it can, prevent the firms from knowing how many bidders they are competing against. This policy can cut two ways. If the actual number of bidders is less than the firms believe it to be, the firms will bid lower than they would bid if they were correctly informed. However, if the firms underestimate the number of their rivals, they will bid high. But the former effect outweighs the latter. This is because of the diminishing returns effect of increasing the number of bidders (see Figures 4.1, 4.2, and 4.3): the more bidders there are, the less each extra bidder drives down the bids. Thus on balance the government's best policy is to keep the number of bidders secret. (We develop this argument in detail in McAfee and McMillan 1987a.)

5. SALES TAXES

Suppose a sales tax is imposed on inputs that a contractor uses. In order to earn as much profit as he would earn in the absence of the sales tax, the contractor will have to raise his bids by an amount equal to the amount he pays in sales tax. If this were the only effect of imposing the tax, it would make no difference to the government whether the contractor paid the tax or not: the revenue the government collected from the sales tax would be exactly matched by the extra amount it would have to pay the contractor.

However, this is not the only effect. The reason why the firms bidding for a given contract generally have different expected costs is that some of the firms expect to use more inputs than the other firms expect to use. Imposing a sales tax raises the expected costs of the high-cost firms by more than it raises the expected costs of the low-cost firms. The variance in the bidders' expected costs increases, which means that bidding competition is reduced: the lowest-cost firm can raise its bid by more than the amount of the sales tax it will pay and still be reasonably confident of winning the contract. Thus the winning firm's expected profit is higher as a result of the imposition of the sales tax.

A surprising conclusion follows. If sales taxes are in force, the government could lower contractors' profits by not requiring firms to pay sales tax on inputs used in government projects. Because such a policy would increase bidding competition, it would lower the government's expected payment to contractors by more than it would lower its revenue from the sales tax. Elimination of the sales tax would result in a net dollar gain to the government.

This conclusion suggests a tentative policy recommendation: the government should rebate taxes paid by contractors on inputs used in government projects.

Some administrative problems might arise in carrying out such a policy. The government would incur auditing costs in checking that items for which a contractor claims sales-tax rebate were in fact used on a government project and not in the contractor's private sector business. However, the collection of sales taxes also involves considerable administrative costs; it is not obvious that exempting certain items from sales taxes would be much more costly administratively than collecting the taxes. In any case, the administrative costs of a rebate scheme would probably be proportionately less important the larger the dollar value of the project. Thus a practical policy recommendation might be that on sufficiently large government projects contractors be allowed to claim a rebate for sales taxes on inputs.

6. BID DISTRIBUTION

The data upon which Tables 4.2 and 4.3 are based can be used to test hypotheses about the nature of the distributions of bids and therefore the nature of the

TABLE 4.5
Tests of hypotheses on bid distributions, Ontario Ministry of Government Services contracts

Contract	Uniform	Exponential
3	Accept	Reject
4	Accept	Reject
5	Reject	Reject
6	Accept	Accept
7	Accept	Reject
8	Accept	Accept
14	Accept	Accept
15	Accept	Reject
16	Reject	Accept
17	Accept	Accept
18	Reject	Accept
19	Accept	Accept

SOURCE: Same as Table 4.2. The confidence level is 99 percent.

distributions of firms' expected costs.

In the special case of the model of McAfee and McMillan (1986) upon which the simulations reported in this chapter and the next chapter are based, we assumed the firms' expected costs were drawn from a uniform distribution. Is this assumption, made for the sake of simplicity in the theory, justified by the data? The first column of Table 4.5 presents results of tests of the hypothesis that the bids come from a uniform distribution: 'accept' means that the hypothesis cannot be rejected and 'reject' means that it is rejected. A caveat is necessary: because of the smallness of the samples (the relatively small number of bidders for any contract), the power of these tests is low. For this reason, the contracts with ten or fewer bidders were not examined.

Table 4.5 also reports the results of tests of the hypothesis that the bids come from an exponential distribution, which we used as an alternative simplifying assumption in the model in McAfee and McMillan (1986) and which has some theoretical justification in that an exponential distribution can be self-sustaining.

The frequency with which the tests accepted the hypothesis that the bid distribution is uniform, together with the extra simplicity the uniform distribution gives to the theory, provides some justification for assuming that bid distributions are uniform when one simulates the effects of varying the characteristics of contracts. Although smallness of the sample sizes may account in part for the high proportion of acceptances, Table 4.5 does at least indicate that postulating a uniform bid distribution is not greatly at variance with the facts.

The assumption that the distribution of bids is uniform is also justified by statistical theory: if all that is known about a distribution is the values of its endpoints, and the endpoints are finite, then the uniform distribution is the distribution with maximum entropy (Theil 1981).

Nevertheless, the assumption of uniform cost distributions is an approximation, and may sometimes not be a good approximation. Thus the empirical estimates reported in this chapter and the next should be interpreted with some caution. Further empirical work on this question is warranted.

Several studies of bidding for mineral rights to land controlled by the US government have found that bids follow an approximately log-normal distribution (Pelto 1971; Ramsey 1983; Reece 1978). However, the mineral-rights problem differs in one fundamental respect from the government-contracting problem. In the government-contracting problem each firm knows its own expected cost: a firm that learns about a rival's expected cost may change its strategic behaviour, but it will not change its perception of its own expected cost. In the mineral-rights problem, the item being bid for has a common true value (namely, the ultimate market value of the mineral), but different bidders have access to different information and so their individual guesses about the actual value of the item are different: learning about a rival's bid may cause a firm to revise its own perception of the item's value. In the terminology of Milgrom and Weber (1982), government-contracting bidding is represented by the independent-private-values model, while mineral-rights bidding is represented by the common-value model. Thus there is little reason to expect the distribution of bids for a government contract to coincide with log-normal.

7. SUMMARY

This chapter has assessed the importance of bidding competition. We have presented data on the effects of competition in reducing the price paid by the government and on the extent of bidding competition in government contracts. Bidding competition can be a powerful force in lowering the price paid by the government. The chapter has suggested four ways in which a government can stimulate bidding competition:(1) by dividing projects into smaller projects and offering a separate contract for each subproject; (2) by exempting contractors from sales taxes on inputs used on government projects; (3) by publicizing the terms of upcoming contract awards as widely as possible to ensure that as many firms as possible are able to submit bids; (4) by publicizing new and superior technologies to reduce the differences between competing firms' costs. Finally, the chapter has tested two hypotheses about the distribution of firms' bids.[4]

4   The foregoing analysis ignored the possibility that bidders might incur significant bid-preparation costs. On the effects of such costs on the optimal number of bidders, see Samuelson (1985).

5

Simulations with Incentive Contracts

The type of contract most commonly used in government contracting is the fixed-price contract. Cost-plus contracts are also often used. The theory developed in this study has shown that, in many circumstances, the government's expected payment would be lower if incentive contracts were used instead. While theoretical analysis can show the existence of potential gains, it cannot establish their size. Are the potential gains from using incentive contracts rather than fixed-price contracts or cost-plus contracts insignificant in practical terms? Or are these potential gains large enough to justify a more frequent use of incentive contracts? This chapter uses data from some actual Ontario government contracts to simulate the effect on the government's payment of changing the form of the contract.

1. DETERMINANTS OF THE OPTIMAL CONTRACT

The simulations are based on the simplest formulation of the optimal-contract analysis. The reader interested in judging the appropriateness of the simplifying assumptions used in the simulations is referred to McAfee and McMillan (1986). Briefly, however, these assumptions are as follows. First, the firms are risk neutral, so the government has nothing to gain from sheltering a firm from risk. Second, the government's auditing is sufficiently frequent and punishment for fraud is sufficiently severe to ensure that firms neither charge the government for materials or labour not used on the project nor overcharge for materials used. Third, the different firms' costs are distributed according to the uniform distribution. Fourth, the moral-hazard effect, which summarizes the contractor's discretionary ability to vary costs by doing the work with more or less efficiency, can be represented by a quadratic function.

Given these simplifying assumptions, the optimal cost-share parameter, α, and therefore the form of the optimal contract, depends on the number of firms that submit bids, the difference between the cost of the highest-cost firm and the cost of the lowest-cost firm (assuming efficient production in each case), and the moral-hazard effect.

This chapter will use data from actual contracts awarded by the Ontario government to simulate what would have happened had the contracts been written differently. Of course, these simulations are meaningful only to the extent that the model upon which they are based approximates the behaviour of real-world firms. Because some of the approximations used may not be good approximations, the empirical results of this chapter should be interpreted with caution. Moreover, the results are likely to become the less reliable the further the extrapolation is from the actual data.[1]

Information on the number of firms bidding is easy to obtain. The use of data on bids actually submitted makes it possible to estimate the highest expected cost and the lowest expected cost that any firm could have (as was done in Chapter 4). It should be stressed that these costs are opportunity costs, as defined in Chapter 2. They include the forgone profits from alternative activities, and they would be low in a recession, when profits from the contractor's other activities would be low.

The only other data needed in order to compute the optimal contract are data on moral hazard; unfortunately, the very nature of moral hazard makes accurate data difficult to obtain.

2. THE SIZE OF THE MORAL-HAZARD EFFECT

In the context of government/firm contracting, moral hazard refers to the extent to which the firm exerts effort to hold down its production costs. The firm can, at some cost not chargeable to the government project, search for lower-priced inputs, resist labour union demands for higher wages, schedule its activities so that no workers will be idle while another part of the project is being completed, manage its raw-material inventories so that no excessive stocks are held, and use only the most efficient number of workers rather than keep on extra workers in the interests of the firm's future activities. A failure to hold down costs is not actually fraudulent, since the firm is not charging the government for expenses it did not incur. But such a failure can markedly raise the cost of the project to the government.

A fixed-price contract gives the firm an adequate incentive to minimize its costs: each extra dollar's worth of expenses incurred by the firm lowers its profit by one dollar. As we argued in the theoretical analysis, however, the fixed-price contract fails to induce much competition among the bidders and forces the contractor to bear all of the risk. A cost-plus contract stimulates more bidding competition and divides the risk, but it gives the contractor no incentive to minimize costs. Thus one measure of the moral-hazard effect is the percentage

1 For a discussion of the pitfalls of simulation studies, see McAfee (1983).

difference between production costs under a cost-plus contract and production costs under a fixed-price contract.

A number of studies of US military contracts have attempted to measure this difference. According to Scherer (1964a: 264), 'casual observation' suggests that costs under a fixed-price contract are typically about 10 per cent lower than costs under a cost-plus contract. Moore (1967: 214) provides a similar estimate, while a study by the General Accounting Office in the mid-1960s (cited in Hiller and Tollison 1978: 242) offers a figure of 5 per cent; however, this figure seems implausibly low.

The difference in behaviour between firms under cost-plus contracts and firms under fixed-price contracts is closely analogous to the difference in behaviour between firms that are under government regulation and firms that are permitted to maximize profits. Consider a firm, such as a telephone company, that has a natural monopoly. A common way in which governments restrain monopoly power is by regulating prices: the firm is required to charge a price that just covers its costs of production plus what is judged to be a fair profit. This form of regulation gives the firm no incentive to minimize its production costs: any cost increase due to inefficient production techniques can be passed on to consumers via a price increase. By contrast, a firm that is allowed to maximize its profits (whether or not it faces competition from other firms) will seek to minimize the cost of producing any given level of output.

The breaking up of the American Telephone and Telegraph Company for antitrust reasons in 1983-84 provides a case study of the effects of regulation on production costs. Immediately after AT&T was forced to compete with other firms, it was observed that the company's workforce was 10 per cent too large. The company had too many layers of management, wages were higher than wages in comparable firms, there was inadequate inventory control, and customers faced long delivery lags. According to an outside observer, AT&T's costs to install and maintain equipment were $61 per hour in 1984, compared with about $30 per hour for its new competitors (*New York Times*, 5 August 1984).

Similarly, the deregulation of the US airline industry revealed that, under regulation, the airlines had been paying wages well above market rates. Wage contracts agreed upon after deregulation often had a two-tier structure, under which new employees sometimes earned only half what the long-standing employees were earning (*New York Times*, 18 November 1984).

Several estimates have been made of the extent to which production costs rise as a result of regulation. For example, a study of US electrical utilities finds that regulation raises production costs by as much as 10 per cent; Koch (1980: 465) states that this estimate is 'consistent with other estimates of the internal inefficiency inspired by regulation.'

The economics of health care provide further evidence of the extent to which costs depend on whether or not the decision-maker bears some responsibility for the costs actually incurred. In the United States, two private sector schemes for financing medical care are fee-for-service arrangements and prepaid group plans. Fee-for-service is an ordinary insurance arrangement: the physician has no incentive to use hospital facilities and other health-care resources efficiently, because all costs are reimbursed by the insurance agency. The fee-for-service arrangement is therefore analogous to a cost-plus contract. Under a prepaid group plan, each consumer pays an annual fee, in return for which the organization provides comprehensive medical care. The economic rationale of the prepaid group plan is that it provides 'the organization and its physicians with a financial incentive to minimize the cost of medical care to its enrollees by allowing it to retain the difference between the capitation payment and the costs of providing medical services' (Feldstein 1983: 327). Under a prepaid group plan, then, the consumer offers the physician a fixed-price contract in return for a specified output—that is, a certain level of health. In practice, prepaid group plans (fixed-price contracts) have considerably lower operating costs than fee-for-service plans (cost-plus contracts). The group plans achieve savings in a variety of ways: by seeking lower-cost hospitals; by reducing the use of facilities that exist primarily for the convenience of the prestige of the physician; by subcontracting for some specialized services to avoid duplication of expensive facilities; by using outpatient care instead of hospitalization when this choice is possible; by making hospital stays shorter; by using auxiliary medical personnel instead of physicians to provide certain services; by providing preventive care and health education programs; and by prescribing generic rather than brand-name drugs. One study finds that the costs of prepaid group plans are, on average, 17 per cent lower than the costs of fee-for-service schemes. Three other studies offer estimates of 27 per cent, 10 per cent, and 25 per cent.[2] The average of these four estimates of the moral-hazard effect is 20 per cent.

The simulations that follow use the figure of 15 per cent as an estimate of how much higher costs are under a cost-plus contract than under a fixed-price contract. However, we shall also investigate the consequences when this figure is either higher or lower.

3. THE SAVINGS FROM USING INCENTIVE CONTRACTS

The contracts to which the data reported in Chapter 4 referred were fixed-price contracts. Most, if not all, of these contracts failed to satisfy the necessary conditions derived in Chapter 3 under which a fixed-price contract is the optimal contract (namely that there are a great many bidders or that all bidders have the same expected cost). The theory therefore suggests that the government could have saved money had it instead used incentive contracts in these instances. How much money could it have saved?

---

2   Feldstein (1983, chap. 12); *New York Times*, 25 November 1984

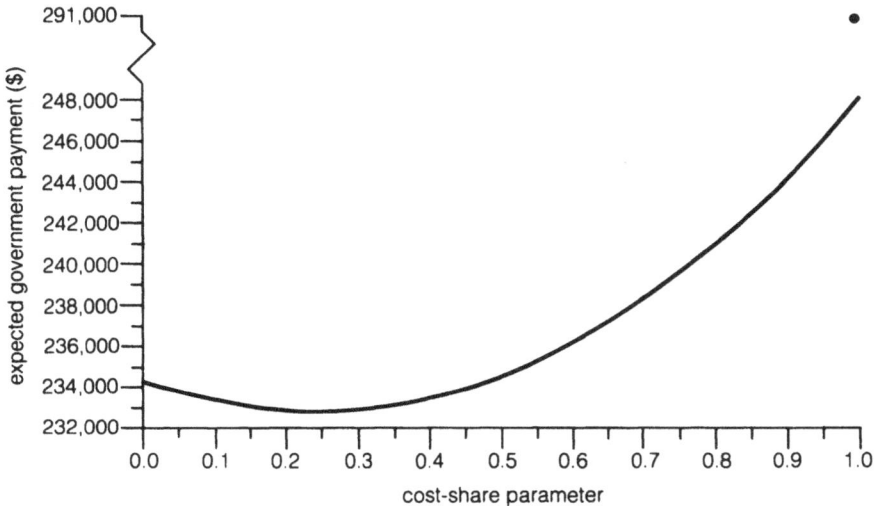

Figure 5.1
Variation of expected government payment with cost-share parameter
SOURCE: Same as Figure 4.1

This question can be answered by using the theoretical analysis in Chapter 3, presuming that the theory models the behaviour of the actual firms with reasonable accuracy.

The relationship between the government's expected payment and the cost-share parameter, α, is plotted in Figures 5.1, 5.2, and 5.3. These figures are based on three actual contracts, arbitrarily selected.

Figure 5.1, which corresponds to the first contract in Table 4.2, shows that the optimal incentive contract in this case has a cost-share parameter, α, of 0.2; had the government used this optimal incentive contract instead of a fixed-price contract, its expected payment would have been $2,005, or 1 per cent, less. Figure 5.2 corresponds to the sixteenth contract in Table 4.4. For this contract, the optimal cost-share parameter is 0.09; using an incentive contract with this cost-share parameter would have saved $479, or 0.15 per cent of total costs. Figure 5.3 corresponds to the twenty-first contract in Table 4.3. The optimal cost-share parameter is 0.99; using this incentive contract would have saved $34,685, or 18 per cent of total costs.

Again, the lowest point on each curve in Figures 5.1, 5.2, and 5.3 shows the value of the cost-share parameter that would minimize the government's expected payment. More generally, the optimal cost-share parameter for any contract can be found by using the analysis in McAfee and McMillan (1986). The results of such an exercise are reported in Tables 5.1, 5.2, and 5.3, which correspond respectively to Tables 4.2, 4.3, and 4.4.

The data in Tables 4.2, 4.3, and 4.4 describe fixed-price contracts. The

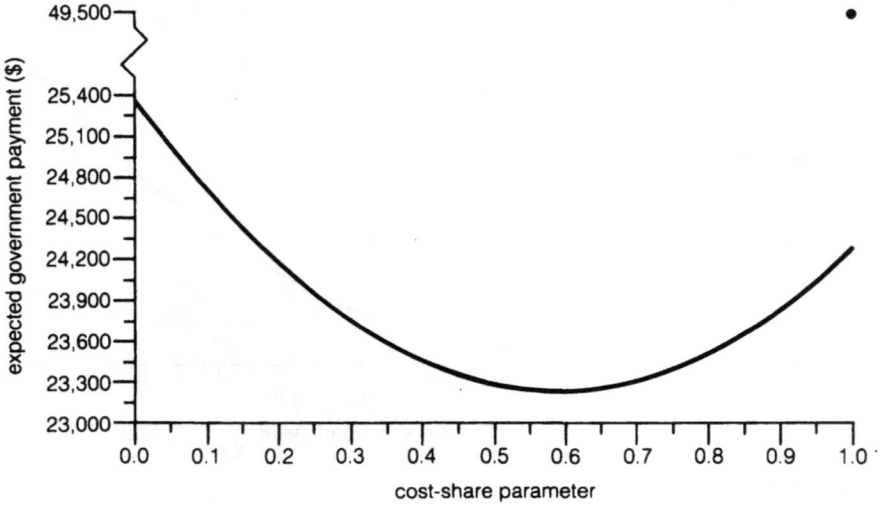

Figure 5.2
Variation of expected government payment with cost-share parameter
SOURCE: Same as Figure 4.2

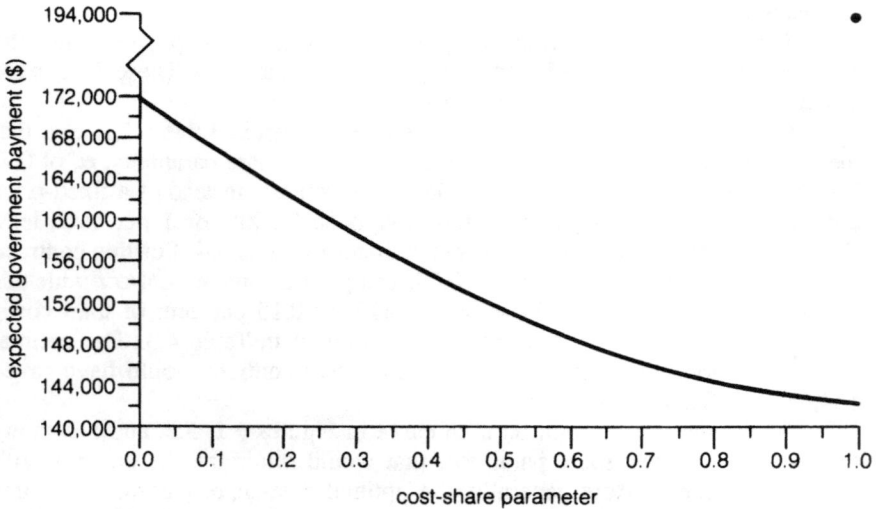

Figure 5.3
Variation of expected government payment with cost-share parameter
SOURCE: Same as Figure 4.3

TABLE 5.1
The optimal cost-share parameter:
Ontario Ministry of Government Services contracts

| Contract | Savings from incentive contract | | Optimal alpha |
	Dollars	Per cent	
1	2,680	1.03	0.22 *
2	2,917	0.12	0.08 *
3	531	0.17	0.09 *
4	108	0.02	0.03 *
5	64	0.11	0.07 *
6	8,785	0.32	0.12 *
7	1,716	0.14	0.08 *
8	3,246	0.65	0.17 *
9	22,740	11.44	0.64
10	5,231	19.45	0.92
11			
12	7,742	1.29	0.24 *
13	4,728	0.53	0.16 *
14	7,292	1.03	0.20 *
15	4,250	1.18	0.21 *
16	2,330	0.66	0.16 *
17	1,369	0.46	0.15 *
18	788	0.23	0.10 *
19	2,705	0.17	0.09 *
20	14,813	2.49	0.32
21	4,512	2.06	0.30

SOURCE: Table 4.2
NOTE: The contracts marked with asterisks are those for which, according to
the rule of thumb suggested in the text, the fixed-price contract was
appropriate.

fourth column of Tables 5.1, 5.2, and 5.3 reports the optimal cost-share
parameter for each of these contracts had they been incentive contracts. The
second and third columns estimate the reduction, in dollar and percentage terms,
in the government's expected payment if the government had used the optimal
incentive contract instead of a fixed-price contract.

For the Ministry of Government Services contracts (Table 5.1), the
computed optimal cost-share parameter varies between 0 and 0.35; the estimated
savings from using the optimal incentive contract range from 0 to 21 per cent,
with an average saving of 2.35 per cent. (Note, with respect to contract 11 in
Table 5.1 and contracts 4, 5, and 22 in Table 5.2, that the computation technique

TABLE 5.2
The optimal cost-share parameter:
Ontario Ministry of Transportation and Communications contracts

| Contract | Savings from incentive contract | | Optimal alpha |
	Dollars	Per cent	
1	7,097	1.03	0.25 *
2	73,909	6.81	0.55
3	2,157	4.46	0.46
4			
5			
6	4,329	2.83	0.40
7	26	0.01	0.03 *
8	48,741	1.18	0.24 *
9	49,052	10.94	0.72
10	3,412	0.32	0.14 *
11	24,044	4.60	0.45
12	5,791	5.33	0.50
13	12,178	34.99	0.99
14	72,131	6.59	0.55
15	121,150	34.11	0.99
16	15,546	3.02	0.38
17	11,951	2.71	0.34
18	4,064	0.25	0.12 *
19	8,284	8.85	0.62
20	1,455	2.61	0.36
21	52,027	26.81	0.99
22			
23	2,198	0.24	0.12 *

SOURCE: Table 4.3
NOTE: The contracts marked with asterisks are those for which, according to the rule of thumb suggested in the text, the fixed-price contract was appropriate.

breaks down when there is only one bidder.) For the Ministry of Transportation and Communications contracts (Table 5.2), the optimal cost-share parameter is between 0 and 0.99; the savings from the incentive contract range from 0 to 35 per cent, with an average of 8.13 per cent. For the Ministry of Natural Resources contracts (Table 5.3), the optimal cost-share parameter varies between 0.24 and 0.99; the savings range from 1 per cent to 68 per cent, with an average of 13.74 per cent. The average saving over all three samples is 8.16 per cent.

Thus the potential for savings is small in the case of the Ministry of Government Services contracts and large in the case of Ministry of Natural

TABLE 5.3
The optimal cost-share parameter:
Ontario Ministry of Natural Resources contracts

Contract	Savings from incentive contract		Optimal alpha
	Dollars	Per cent	
1	32,723	20.40	0.85
2	236,806	68.30	0.99
2*	148,191	45.04	0.99
3	1,980	0.87	0.22 *
4	4,733	3.60	0.44
5	32,492	27.68	0.66
6	31,873	21.87	0.80
7	11,703	2.94	0.40
8	71,387	4.17	0.35
9	20,750	2.50	0.30 *
10	16,734	9.64	0.50
11	5,433	4.46	0.41
12	8,723	4.35	0.44
13	24,007	14.93	0.76
14	2,326	9.20	0.47
15	3,301	8.69	0.49
16	3,909	12.41	0.54
17	2,793	15.96	0.67
18	1,556	4.42	0.39
19	1,973	5.23	0.40
20	3,428	1.42	0.24 *

SOURCE: Table 4.4
NOTE: The contracts marked with asterisks are those for which, according to the rule of thumb suggested in the text, the fixed-price contract was appropriate.

Resources contracts. However, it does not follow that the former ministry's current procedures are better than the latter's. For most of the Ministry of Natural Resources contracts, the number of bidders was relatively small and the bids were widely dispersed (compare Table 4.2 with Table 4.4). These are the ideal circumstances in which to use incentive contracts, since in these circumstances there are large gains to be had from using the cost-share parameter to stimulate bidding competition. (Indeed, it can be tentatively concluded from these data—perhaps surprisingly—that the dispersion of the bidders' production costs is a more important determinant of the extent of bidding competition than is the number of bidders.)

Tables 5.1, 5.2, and 5.3 show that when the computed optimal cost-share parameter is less than 0.3 the percentage savings are small, less than 2 per cent. Given that an incentive contract generates slightly higher administrative costs than does a fixed-price contract (see Chapter 3), a rule of thumb might be to use a fixed-price contract when the optimal cost-share parameter is less than 0.3. The projects for which, given this rule, the use of a fixed-price contract was appropriate are marked with asterisks in Tables 5.1, 5.2, and 5.3. For the remaining projects, the average saving from a switch to an incentive contract would have been 13.1 per cent and the average value of the optimal cost-share parameter would have been 0.61. The choice of a fixed-price contract was optimal, according to our rule of thumb, in 40 per cent of the cases examined. In the remaining cases, using an incentive contract would have significantly lowered the government's contracting costs.

Several of the estimated optimal contracts in Tables 5.1, 5.2, and 5.3 have values of α very close to 1.0; that is, the optimal contract is an incentive contract that is close to a cost-plus contract. (In Tables 5.1, 5.2, and 5.3, the optimal α for these contracts is reported as 0.99; 0.90 might be better in practice, since it is more clearly different from 1.0.) As long as α is less than 1.0, bids are related to true expected costs, so that the lowest-cost firm reveals itself by submitting the lowest bid. If there are very few bidders, or if the bidders' costs are widely dispersed, then it is in the government's interest to set α close to 1.0; the government's gains from stimulating bidding competition outweigh its losses arising from the contractor's lack of incentives to hold his costs down. This explains why some of the estimated optimal contracts are close to (but not exactly) cost-plus.

4. CHANGES IN THE PARAMETERS

The theoretical analysis in Chapter 3 showed that the optimal value of the cost-share parameter, α, depends on three factors: the number of firms submitting bids, the difference between the expected cost of the highest-cost firm and the expected costs of the lowest-cost firm, and the extent of moral hazard. How sensitive in practice is the value of the optimal cost-share parameter to changes in any of these parameters?

Figures 5.4, 5.5, and 5.6 plot the variation of the optimal cost-share parameter with the number of bidders. The data on expected costs come from the three actual contracts investigated earlier. For the moral-hazard effect, we use the 15 per cent estimate discussed earlier in this chapter. Figures 5.4, 5.5, and 5.6 show that the more bidders there are the closer the optimal contract is to a fixed-price contract ($\alpha = 0$). This result follows because the more bidders there are the stronger the bidding competition is, and therefore the less need there is to use the cost-share parameter to stimulate bidding competition.

Figures 5.7, 5.8, and 5.9 plot the variation of the optimal cost-share parameter with the ratio of the highest possible cost to the lowest possible cost.

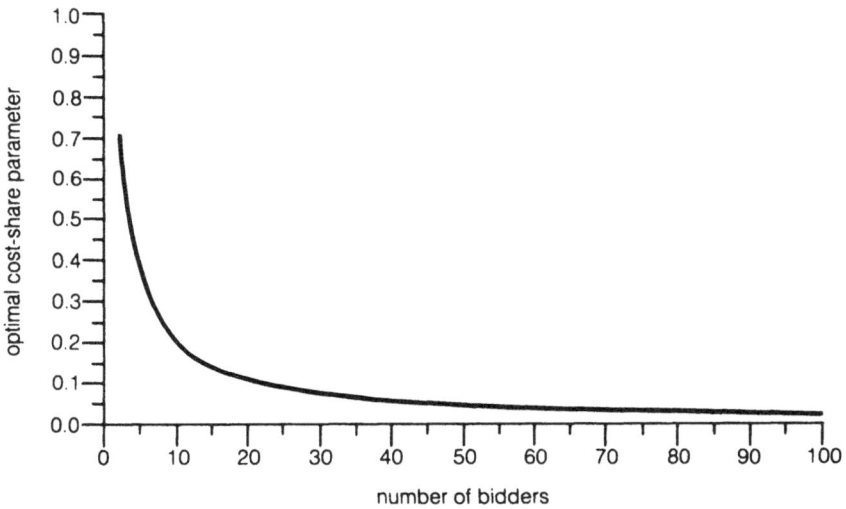

Figure 5.4
Variation of optimal cost-share parameter with number of bidders
SOURCE: Same as Figure 4.1

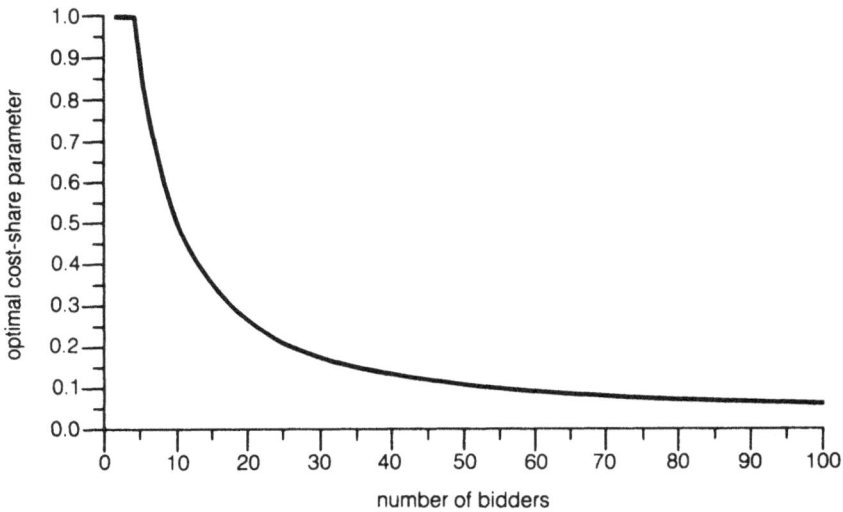

Figure 5.5
Variation of optimal cost-share parameter with number of bidders
SOURCE: Same as Figure 4.2

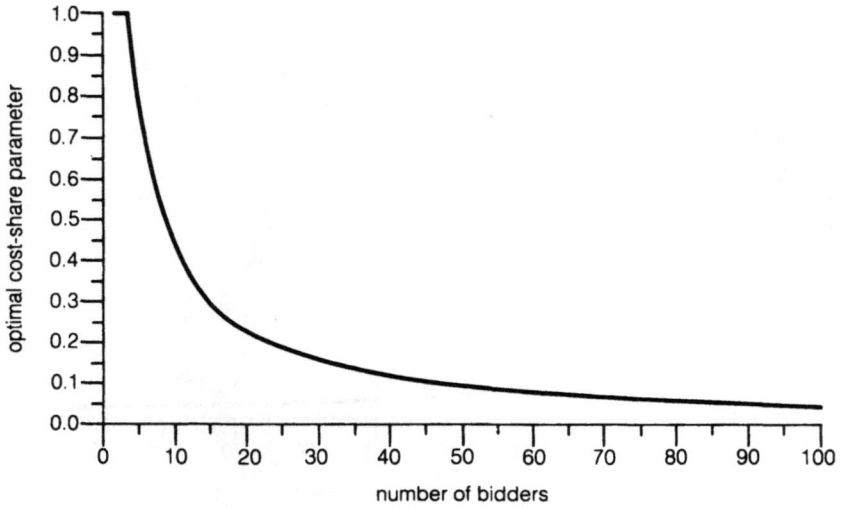

Figure 5.6
Variation of optimal cost-share parameter with number of bidders
SOURCE: Same as Figure 4.3

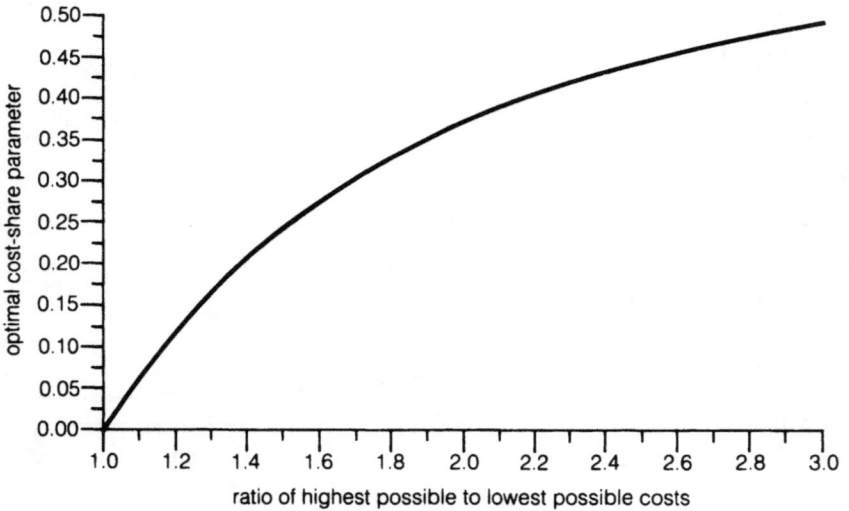

Figure 5.7
Variation of optimal cost-share parameter with dispersion of expected costs
SOURCE: Same as Figure 5.4

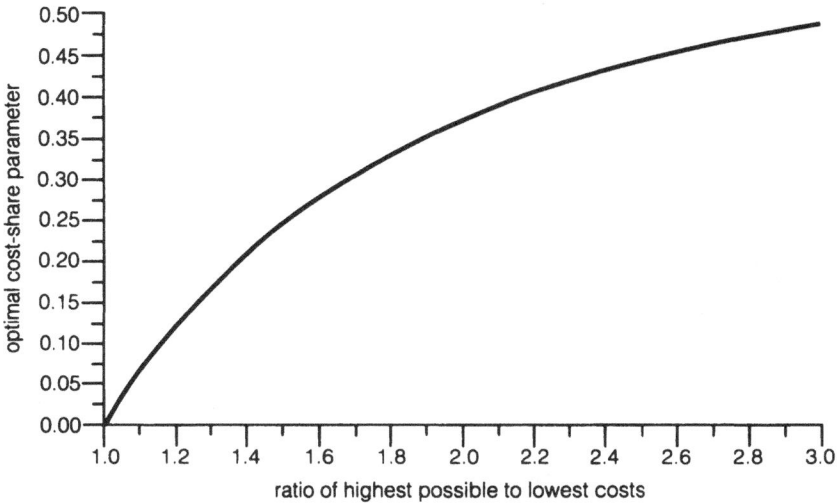

Figure 5.8
Variation of optimal cost-share parameter with dispersion of expected costs
SOURCE: Same as Figure 5.5

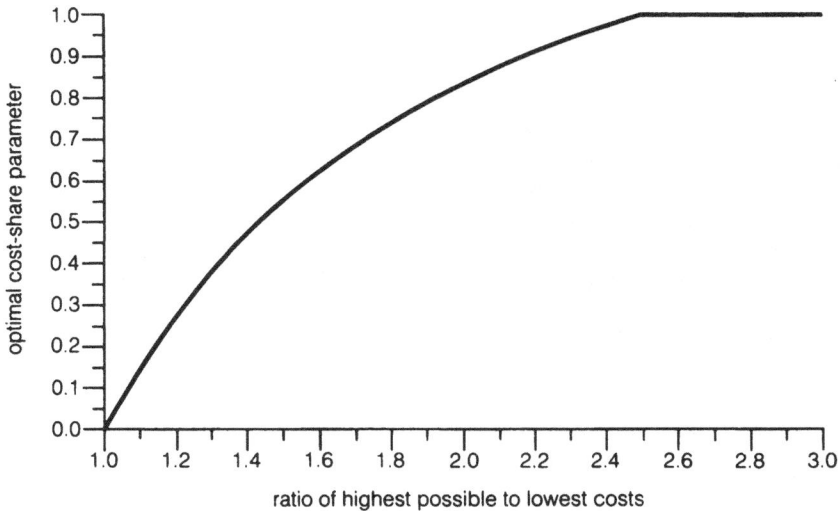

Figure 5.9
Variation of optimal cost-share parameter with dispersion of expected costs
SOURCE: Same as Figure 5.6

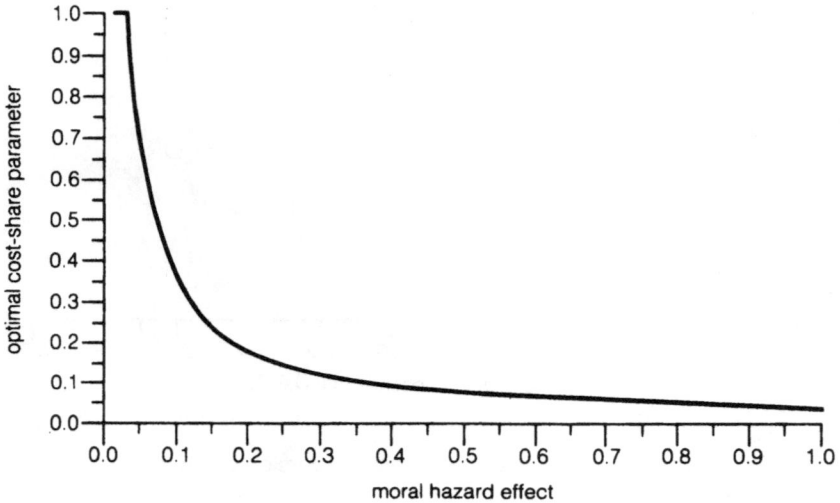

Figure 5.10
Variation of optimal cost-share parameter with moral-hazard opportunities
SOURCE: Same as Figure 5.4

Data on the number of bidders and the lowest possible cost come from the three actual contracts mentioned earlier, and we use the 15 per cent figure for moral hazard; we allow the highest possible cost to vary between being equal to the lowest possible cost and being three times the lowest possible cost. The smaller the difference is between highest possible cost and lowest possible cost, the closer the optimal contract is to a fixed-price contract, since the smaller this difference is the more bidding competition there is.

Figures 5.10, 5.11, and 5.12 depict the variation in the optimal cost-share parameter with the moral-hazard effect. Data on number of bidders and expected costs are taken from the same three contracts. We vary the moral-hazard effect between 1 per cent (which means that production costs are typically 1 per cent higher under a cost-plus contract than they are under a fixed-price contract) and 50 per cent (which means that costs are typically 50 per cent higher under a cost-plus contract than they are under a fixed-price contract). The more marked the moral-hazard effect is, the closer the optimal incentive contract is to a fixed-price contract, since the stronger moral hazard is the more important it is to give the contractor incentives to keep costs low.

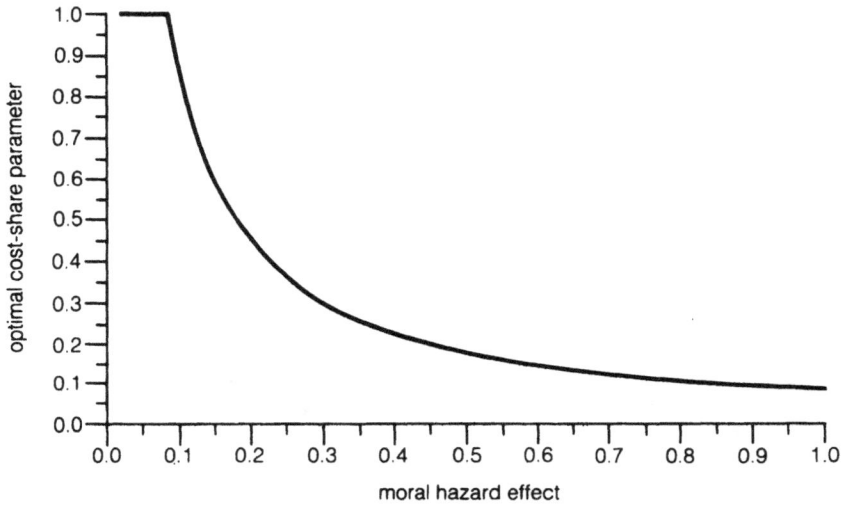

Figure 5.11
Variation of optimal cost-share parameter with moral-hazard opportunities
SOURCE: Same as Figure 5.5

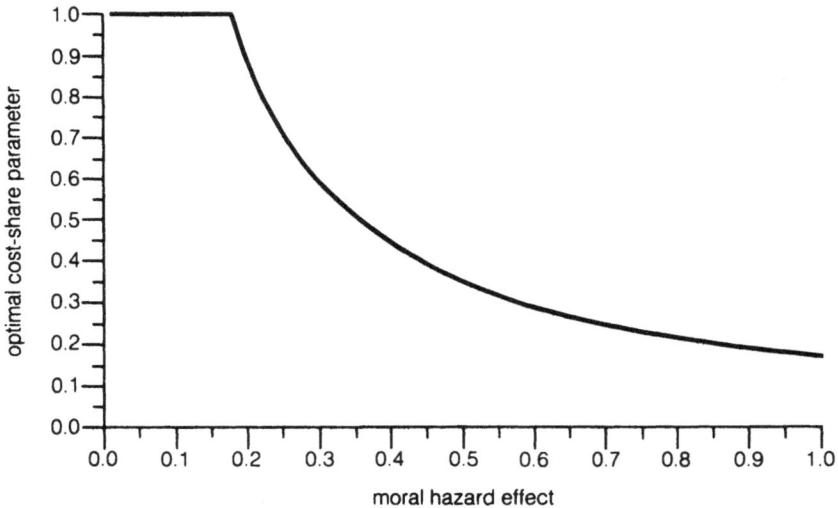

Figure 5.12
Variation of optimal cost-share parameter with moral-hazard opportunities
SOURCE: Same as Figure 5.6

5. CRITICISMS OF INCENTIVE CONTRACTS

A government need not change the form of the contracts it uses in order to achieve savings. It can save money in a number of other ways, such as by using competitive procurement where it now uses sole-source procurement, or by making sure that the criteria for a project's success are unambiguous. In other words, we do not claim that incentive contracts are a panacea for government contracting problems. We simply suggest that the systematic use of incentive contracts is one way of lowering contracting costs.

Fox (1984: 67-9) cites three practical objections to the use of incentive contracts. First, difficulties 'arise from frequent changes in the work statement, the allowable costs, and the incentive fee as a result of unexpected technical developments, new government requirements, or other factors.' Second, 'when profit is a function of the way the work is performed, contractors may resist direction from the customer. Moreover, even in those few instances where incentives motivate program goals, the risk of technical performance failure increases.' Third, 'to allow for uncertainties that may reduce profit or affect cost reimbursement, a prudent contractor will include a much larger contingency in a bid for an incentive contract than for a cost-reimbursement contract.'

None of these points damages the case for using incentive contracts. The first criticism does not apply to incentive contracts as such: any kind of contract—fixed-price, cost-plus, or incentive—will cause problems if its initial technical specifications are inadequate. Like the first criticism, the second is really about the government's administration of contracts: if the contractor's work is inadequate, he should suffer some penalty; again the nature of the contract is beside the point. The third objection is correct but irrelevant because, as we argued in Chapter 3, the bids for a cost-plus contract are meaningless. The higher profit rate associated with an incentive contract is counteracted by the stronger incentives for the firm to hold its costs down and by the fact that the use of an incentive contract rather than a cost-plus contract means that the most efficient firm reveals itself in the initial bidding.

Fox's solution to the problem of cost increases, namely that the government 'must offer contractors much higher profits in return for reduced costs,' is one of the effects that incentive contracts are designed to have.

A number of econometric studies of US Department of Defense contracting experience (experience that we shall discuss in some detail in the next chapter) have estimated small or nonexistent savings from incentive contracts relative to cost-plus contracts (Cross 1968; Fisher 1969; Hiller and Tollison 1978). However, these studies do not provide an argument against using the incentive contract, because they compared non-optimal incentive contracts with cost-plus contracts. Incentive contracts have not as yet been applied after systematic consideration of their effects on the firms' cost control, on the bidding competition, and on the sharing of risks; instead, the cost-share parameter has been chosen in an arbitrary fashion. It is possible for an arbitrarily chosen incentive contract to be more costly to the government than a fixed-price contract or a cost-plus contract.

The studies cited above also failed to take account of what the present analysis has identified as the main failing of cost-plus contracts: the fact that, unlike bids for incentive contracts or fixed-price contracts, bids for cost-plus contracts are not related to expected production costs, so that in all likelihood the most efficient firm is not awarded the contract. Figures 5.1, 5.2, and 5.3 show, by the discontinuity at $\alpha = 1$, that this effect can cause a cost-plus contract to be much more costly than an incentive contract.

6. SUMMARY

This chapter has supplemented the theoretical analysis of the optimal incentive contract by investigating the quantitative significance of the determinants of the optimal contract. We have given some estimates of both the likely size of the moral-hazard effect and the savings that can be realized by using incentive contracts instead of fixed-price contracts; the average saving in our sample was over 8 per cent. The chapter also investigated the extent to which the optimal cost-share parameter varies with the underlying parameters.

The computations reported in this chapter illustrate how an approximately optimal contract can be implemented in practice. The data requirements are not severe: the decision-maker must predict the likely number of bidders, the likely highest and lowest bids, and the size of the moral-hazard effect. Nor are the computational requirements severe: the computation of the optimal cost-share parameter can be done quickly on a hand calculator.

APPENDIX

To do the computations reported in this chapter, we simplified the formulae in McAfee and McMillan (1986) by assuming that the firms are risk neutral, their expected costs are distributed uniformly on $[c_1, c_2]$, and the cost incurred by the contractor in reducing his production cost by y is $y^2/2d$ for some constant d which, under these assumptions, can be shown to equal the difference between production cost under a cost-plus contract and under a fixed-price contract). In particular, the optimal level of the sharing parameter is calculated as $\alpha^* = (c_2 - c_1)/(n + 1)d$, where n is the number of bidders, provided this implies an α^* less than one. (This follows from Theorem 2 of McAfee and McMillan [1986].)

6

United States Military Contracting

The theoretical analysis in Chapter 3 suggested that the optimal contract will often be an incentive contract. At present, the agency that makes the most extensive use of incentive contracts is the United States Department of Defense (DOD). The experience of this agency provides an instructive case study of contracting problems.[1]

The amounts of money spent on US military contracts are huge. In 1984, the United States spent $220 billion on the military. The object of the fastest growing part of this expenditure was procurement, mostly of weapons: $64 billion was spent on procurement in 1984, and this figure is projected to rise to $107 billion in 1987.

Military contracting in the United States has been a matter of so much discussion that it has added some new expressions to the English language. The term 'military-industrial complex' goes back to Eisenhower's presidency. A more recent addition to the language is 'Beltway bandits.' The Capital Beltway is a highway that encircles Washington, DC. The Beltway bandits are scientific and engineering firms, often staffed by former government officials, that seem to be especially adept at securing government consultancy contracts.

1. THE AWARDING OF CONTRACTS

The Department of Defense uses three different methods to procure weapons systems. First, there is sole-source negotiation. The contracting officers

---

1   This chapter draws heavily on Fox (1974) and DeMayo (1983). It also uses information from Boger, Jones, and Sontheimer (1983), Cross (1968), Cummins (1977), Danhof (1968), Fishe and McAfee (1982), Fisher (1969), Fox (1984), Gansler (1980), Hiller and Tollison (1978), Moore (1967), Scherer (1964a, 1964b), Steinberg (1984), Yuspeh (1976), and articles in the *New York Times*: 11 March 1984, 19 March 1984, 25 March 1984, 1 April 1984, 8 July 1984, 22 July 1984, 5 August 1984, 15 August 1984, 23 September 1984, 10 January 1985, 27 March 1985, 29 March 1985, 31 March 1985; the *Globe and Mail*: 6 June 1984; the *Toronto Star*: 30 June 1984; the *Los Angeles Times*: 24 and 27 November 1984; *Aviation Week and Space Technology*: 26 November 1984, 7 January 1985; and *Newsweek*: 11 February 1985.

negotiate the contract price with a single producer. A mutually acceptable price is agreed upon, based on the contractor's cost estimates. (Notice that the government is at a disadvantage in these negotiations, since the contractor's information about the likely costs is much better than the government's.) The second procurement method is competitive negotiation. The DOD contacts several potential producers, rather than just one, and requests bids from the selected firms. The department does not necessarily choose the lowest bid; a judgment is made by the DOD officials about how high the technological quality of each firm's product is likely to be. The third method is advertised bidding. Any contractor may submit a bid; the DOD is required by law to accept the lowest bid.

The Department of Defense has not taken full advantage of the savings to be had from competitive procurement; instead, it has tended to use sole-source procurement for most major weapons systems. Through the 1960s and 1970s, 10-12 per cent of military prime contract awards were formally advertised, 27-33 per cent were solicited competitively from multiple sources, and 50-60 per cent were solicited from a sole source. These numbers underestimate the extent of sole-source contracting, since the DOD has generally used competitive contracting for contracts of smaller values than those it has awarded on a sole-source basis. Between 1979 and 1981, the proportion of contracts let by competitive bidding fell from 7.9 per cent to 4.1 per cent. (See Table 4.1 for evidence on the relative costs of sole-source and competitive procurement in military contracts.)

However, it is not always feasible or desirable to use open competitive bidding. Many Department of Defense contracts involve competition over design as well as price. Evaluating the bids in such a case can be an expensive exercise: for one Air Force contract, government personnel spent 182,000 man-hours in evaluating the bids from four prospective contractors. For contracts of this kind, it is obviously appropriate to limit the competition. (In McAfee and McMillan [1987b], we develop a theoretical analysis of optimal bidding procedures when the evaluation of bids is costly.)

In order to avoid being trapped in a sole-source position, the Department of Defense has begun to use what it calls 'dual sourcing'; that is, ordering the same weapons system from more than one firm. For example, Pratt and Whitney was originally (from 1974) the only manufacturer of the F-100 engine for the F-15 and F-16 fighter aircraft. Beginning in 1979, the Air Force encouraged another firm, General Electric, to develop the capability of building a similar engine by paying $300 million of General Electric's development costs. The production contracts were then split between the two firms: in 1985 Pratt and Whitney was awarded 25 per cent of the work (down from 100 per cent); its share for 1986 was 46 per cent. The Air Force estimates that its savings from lower bids and improved quality resulting from the presence of competition could eventually amount to $3 billion to $4 billion over the twenty-year lifespan of this type of engine.

2. MORAL HAZARD AND COST CONTROL

The theoretical analysis in Chapter 3 distinguished two ways in which the contracting firm can influence the costs it incurs. First, the firm can, at some cost to itself not chargeable to the government project, lower its costs. Second, it can charge costs to the government project at an artificially high rate.

One way in which a firm can cut its costs for a particular project is by eliminating some of its currently surplus personnel, equipment, or research activity. The cost of doing this is the harm it does to the firm's future competitive position and thus to its future sales. It is DOD practice to place considerable weight on the availability of experienced manpower when it selects a contractor for a new project; hence a firm that reduces its current costs by reducing the number of people it employs can reduce its chances of winning future contracts.

Another way in which a firm can affect its costs by its own efforts is by choosing the amount of planning it undertakes before work on the project begins; the more planning it undertakes, the lower is the probability that costly restarts will be necessary.

A contracting firm can also make more or less of an effort to control the wages it pays to its workers. If the firm can pass any cost increases on to the government, it is likely to buy labour peace by offering higher wages; in contrast, a firm that bears the responsibility for its own costs is more likely to resist labour-union wage demands. According to Pentagon data, the average basic wage of workers in the aerospace industry is 38 per cent higher than the average for all US manufacturing workers. And according to a General Accounting Office study, executives of the large military aerospace contractors receive in salary and non-cash benefits 42 per cent more on average than do executives in business firms in general.

The firm may be able to shift overhead costs from other current projects to the government project. For example, an aircraft manufacturer might apply elements of a given design to both its civilian and its military aircraft, while charging the whole cost of the design process to the military project. Alternatively, the firm might use the current government contract to pay not just for the current work, but also for investment in new equipment or for the training of new personnel; this practice will lower the firm's costs and make it more competitive in bidding for future government or private-sector projects.

The foregoing examples illustrate moral hazard: a firm may not do its best to achieve efficient production if it gains something from the inefficiency. No outright fraud is involved, however, because all of the costs that the firm charges to the government are in fact incurred, albeit unnecessarily.

Fraud is also a problem in military contracting: it has been estimated that fraud costs the Department of Defense several billion dollars a year.

One example of fraudulent activity is billing for work actually done by low-level technicians at the much higher rate of senior scientists or engineers. Labour costs are mischarged in other ways as well. For example, in March 1985 a US federal grand jury indicted the General Electric Company on charges that it had falsified claims for work on a nuclear warhead system. It was alleged that the government had been defrauded of at least $800,000 between January 1980 and April 1983 because the company had entered exaggerated charges on employee time cards.

Another form of cost padding consists of deliberately failing to satisfy the project's specifications. In 1984 the National Semiconductor Corporation was fined $1.75 million for delivering semiconductor chips that had not been tested to the extent required by the contract. The military specifications required that the chips be tested for defective circuits by running electricity through them for nearly seven days. The firm was found to have frequently run the test for only two days, thereby shortening production times and lowering production costs.

Overcharging for inputs used is another way in which contractors can inflate their costs. In 1984 an audit by the DOD's inspector-general found that contractors were often charging the government hundreds of dollars for spare parts and tools that could be obtained for a fraction of the cost if they were ordered from public catalogues. The audit found that 36 per cent of the parts sampled were overpriced, although the overpricing amounted in total to only 6 per cent of the value of the equipment in question. Reports of contractors' overcharging the Pentagon appear regularly: thus it has been claimed that hammers selling for $7 in hardware stores were charged to the DOD at $436; that a small plastic cap worth 75 cents was charged at $1,118 per unit; that a 25-cent plastic washer was charged at $400 per unit. In 1984, the Air Force paid $7,600 for a coffee maker for use in a Lockheed transport aircraft. These inflated prices are in part a consequence of the Pentagon's accounting rules: a large proportion of the price of the $436 hammer consists of overhead and extra labour costs charged in accordance with Pentagon regulations. (As we pointed out in Chapter 3, however, popular concern about such overcharging may be misdirected: the overcharging may be cancelled out by the bidding competition and thus does not necessarily raise the cost of the project to the government.)

The general overseeing of contract performance and the investigation of fraud are the responsibility of the Department of Defense itself and of the General Accounting Office, an investigatory arm of Congress. In the 1983-84 fiscal year, the DOD obtained 657 convictions for fraud by contractors, involving over $14 million in fines, restitutions, and recoveries.

3. PROBLEMS WITH CONTRACTS

One problem associated with contracts has been the difficulty of making the bid price or target price meaningful. According to one observer, 'Established defense companies compete fiercely for new contracts. They inevitably promise maximum performance for minimum price, knowing from experience that once a contract is won, they can negotiate contract changes to cover cost overruns, schedule delays, and reduction in weapon performance. Traditionally, companies have been relieved of contract obligations by the Defense Department when unable to meet them' (Fox 1974: 467). This willingness on the government's part to change the terms of a contract obviously negates the usefulness of any cost-reduction incentives built into the original contract.

The government's readiness to renegotiate contracts may also mean that the bidding process will not reveal the lowest-cost firm. Provided that the final payment to the firm depends on the amount the firm bids, the lowest-cost firm bids lowest. But if the bid is irrelevant to the determination of the final payment, firms have an incentive to bid unrealistically low simply in order to win the contract. In these circumstances, picking the firm that bids lowest will not necessarily result in the most efficient firm's being chosen. In 1981 the Hughes Aircraft Company made a contract with the Air Force to produce prototypes of an advanced medium-range air-to-air missile, the Amraam. Production delays of several months meant that the contract had to be renegotiated upwards by an estimated $100 million. According to an Air Force spokesman, 'the contractor gave us a success-oriented schedule that was too optimistic.'

A second reason why firms sometimes bid lower than their true expected costs is that one contract often follows another. For example, a development contract may be followed by a contract to produce the newly developed item. A firm may bid low and possibly accept low profits on the development contract in order to be in a sole-source position for the subsequent production contracts. The firm can then exploit its monopoly power to earn high profits. This tendency is reinforced by the fact that most development contracts, because of the large risk associated with them, are cost-plus contracts, so that the true expected costs have little relevance to the choice of how low to bid.

Cost overruns are a frequent source of popular concern about US military contracting. According to one estimate, 90 per cent of the major weapons systems procured by the US military cost at least twice as much as they were originally expected to cost. Thus the cost of the F-111 aircraft increased from an original estimate of $2.8 million per unit in 1962 to $14.7 million per unit in 1970. Not coincidentally, there were 1,500 negotiated changes in the F-111 contract during 1967 and 1968 alone, an average of two changes per day. These changes resulted in a total cost increase of $1.5 billion.

The deputy secretary of defence said in 1983 that poor workmanship added from 10 to 30 per cent to the cost of procuring weapons systems. Some of the problems were as elementary as faulty soldering and incorrect colour-coding of wires. The DOD's budget for the 1984-85 fiscal year outlined a 'wide-ranging program' to improve quality and reduce maintenance expenses. Under this new program, Pentagon inspectors examine the work being done in contractors' factories, trying to catch flaws in manufacturing. The program also provides incentives to contractors to upgrade their quality control. In addition, the Pentagon has begun to enforce the quality-control provisions in its contracts more strictly. In August 1984, the Navy refused, on the grounds of 'marginal workmanship,' to accept delivery of Phoenix air-to-air missiles from the Hughes

Aircraft Company and threatened to look for an alternative firm to build the missile. The Navy withheld payments worth $45 million for three months, then resumed full contract payments and began to accept deliveries again, on the grounds that 'Hughes has been fully responsive in establishing corrective action for the quality deficiencies that have been identified by the Navy.'

In 1983 Congress passed a law that requires the manufacturers of weapons procured by the Department of Defense to guarantee that their products will in fact work. The passage of the law was opposed by the DOD, which argued that the department is better able to bear risks than are the contracting firms. The DOD claimed that requiring the firms to bear risks by requiring weapons warranties would raise the cost to the DOD of procuring weapons. (The DOD's argument is valid if the contracting firms can be presumed to be risk averse: see the general analysis in Chapter 2.)

4. FIXED-PRICE CONTRACTS AND COST-PLUS CONTRACTS

The fixed-price contract, while it has the disadvantages that it induces too little bidding competition and requires the firms to bear all of the risk, has the advantage that it provides strong incentives for cost control: the firm itself bears the full burden of any cost overrun. This advantage can be lost if the contract is badly administered, as has sometimes been the case in US military contracting. Thus the practice of making frequent changes in the specifications of the project can in effect convert a fixed-price contract into a cost-plus contract. Again, a vaguely specified project, without precise, objective criteria for success, is effectively a cost-plus contract even if it is nominally fixed-price. A textbook for military-contract negotiators illustrates this point by advising firms always to accept any research contract, even if it is fixed-price: 'Negotiate a statement of work or specification so broad that delivery of the contract end item (usually a feasibility report or at most a prototype) would be acceptable whatever may be the result of the research. Who can challenge the effectiveness of a study, system, model, or report? The report could be nothing more than a paragraph indicating that the research reached a dead end not meriting the expenditure of more funds' (quoted in Fox 1974: 237).

Military research and development spending in the United States amounted to over $29 billion in 1984 (nearly one-third of total US research and development expenditure). Research and development contracts are often, though not always, cost-plus contracts, a choice that the DOD justifies on the grounds that research and development involve considerable uncertainty. Profit under a cost-plus contract is a function of the costs estimated before work starts on the project; the contractor bears no risk and therefore has no incentive to minimize costs.

The lack of such an incentive has a variety of bad effects: contractors fail to plan adequately, wasting money on false starts and dead ends; the firm assigns its most qualified people to projects where performance determines profits, and only inferior workers are left for the cost-plus project; overhead costs, which are difficult for the government to monitor, are inflated; the contractor often overestimates his technical capabilities or underestimates his costs, for he can do so without penalty. Yet these problems are by no means a necessary consequence of research and development contracting: the analysis in Chapter 3 showed that large uncertainty does not justify using a cost-plus contract, since an incentive contract with a cost-share parameter of just less than 1 will virtually eliminate the contractor's risk without eliminating his incentive to minimize costs.

The Department of Defense routinely links contract prices to the inflation rate. Increases in materials and labour prices during the production period are reimbursed in accordance with Bureau of Labor Statistics price indexes, which are established in the contract. Thus the risk of inflationary price increases is not borne by the firm. For example, in January 1985 the Air Force negotiated a $439 million reduction in the price of its contract with Lockheed Corporation for the production of fifty C-5B transport aircraft. The original contract, signed in 1982, was a fixed-price contract totalling $7.8 billion. However, actual inflation rates over the period of the contract were lower than the projected inflation rates on which the original cost calculations were based. Hence the fixed price was adjusted downwards. (See Chapter 3 for a discussion of contingent contracts.)

5. EXPERIENCE WITH INCENTIVE CONTRACTS

Incentive contracts first became widely used in US military contracting in the early 1960s, in response to alarm about the magnitude and frequency of cost overruns on cost-plus contracts. In 1961 less than one-sixth of all large military contracts were incentive contracts; by 1980 the ratio had risen to one-third. It is the current policy of the United States Navy to use incentive contracts for shipbuilding. The production of most Department of Defense weapons systems is carried out under incentive contracts. Cost-plus contracts are now mainly limited to projects with large uncertainty, such as research and development projects associated with new weapons systems and aerospace projects.

Experience has shown that cost overruns are much less frequent and much smaller under incentive contracts than they are under cost-plus contracts. In November 1984, Secretary of the Navy John Lehman stated that 'we are achieving, through our procurement reforms, substantial underruns.' However, as the theoretical analysis pointed out, cost underruns do not necessarily imply that the government has achieved substantial cost savings. Because the incentive contract produces weaker bidding competition and requires the contractor to bear more risk than does the cost-plus contract, the bid or target cost, in comparison with which cost overruns are computed, is higher under an incentive contract than it is under a cost-plus contract.

In early 1985, Secretary of Defense Caspar Weinberger was advocating the use of incentive contracts with a cost-share parameter of 0.5. The advantage of incentive contracts, he was reported as saying, is that the contractors 'get a somewhat higher profit, and we get a [weapon] for less money.'

Two types of incentive contract are used by the Department of Defense. The fixed-price incentive contract sets an upper limit on the government's payment; if the contractor's costs exceed this limit, the contract works like a fixed-price contract. The cost-plus-incentive-fee contract, in contrast, has no upper limit.

Since incentive contracts make payment depend on the contractor's cost, there is a need for some auditing of firms' cost statements. Thus incentive contracts are somewhat more costly for the government to administer than are fixed-price contracts. However, they need not be as costly to administer as cost-plus contracts. Because an incentive contract forces the contractor to bear part of the responsibility for his own costs, it gives him less of an incentive to inflate his costs than does a cost-plus contract. Thus, as we argued in Chapter 3, a relatively low probability of audit is sufficient to deter cost padding under incentive contracts. This conclusion is in fact in accord with Department of Defense practice: the government does less auditing of firms with incentive contracts than it does of firms with cost-plus contracts. To quote a Brookings Institution study of US government contracting: 'A cost-plus-fixed-fee contract ... imposes upon the government the need to assure itself that the contractor's operations are efficiently and economically conducted. This has meant elaborate reporting requirements and auditing procedures that have been costly to the government and irritating to business management. With the incentive contract, the government has less need of such controls and some reduction in their application has occurred. Further reduction is taking place as the government applies its policy of relying more fully upon cost considerations. As incentive contracts impose greater cost consciousness upon management, the government is moving toward a reduction of its review and overhead audit controls' (Danhof 1968: 167-8).

The increasing use of incentive contracts by the Department of Defense over the past twenty years demonstrates the success of this contract form. When Robert S. McNamara was secretary of defence in the 1960s, he claimed that using an incentive contract instead of a cost-plus contract resulted in average cost savings for the government of 10 per cent. Given the large sums of money involved, 10 per cent translates into a large dollar saving. Some observers have suggested that this figure is too high, and the imperfect nature of the available data means that no estimate can be put forward with complete confidence. However, the simulations reported in Chapter 5 suggest that 10 per cent may actually underestimate the savings obtainable from ceasing to use cost-plus contracts.

6. CHOICE OF THE SHARING PARAMETER

There is a sense in which military contracting experience in the United States is of only limited relevance to an evaluation of the cost-saving potential of incentive contracts. If a government is to achieve maximum cost savings, its choice of a cost-share parameter—that is, its choice of the proportions in which cost overruns will be shared between the government and the contractor—must be optimal. If a fixed-price contract is not optimal in a given context, an incentive contract, with some particular cost-share parameter, must be optimal. There is no guarantee that an incentive contract with an arbitrarily chosen cost-share parameter will perform better than a fixed-price contract or a cost-plus contract. (Figures 5.1, 5.2, and 5.3 show how much higher the government's expected payment can be if the government chooses the wrong cost-share parameter.)

The value of the cost-share parameter used in US military contracts varies between 0.5 and 0.9; 0.8 is typical. The government specifies the cost-share parameter when it solicits proposals from potential contractors for target costs and target profits. How is the cost-share parameter used in a given contract determined? While information on this point is difficult to obtain, it appears that the cost-share parameter is normally chosen in an unsystematic way. The executive director for contracts in the Naval Air Systems Command of the United States Navy makes this point: 'While published literature on incentive contracts provides some general guidance on allocation of cost risk on an equitable basis, there is no known source of information that deals with sensitivity analysis aspects of sharing arrangements to assist in award decisions' (DeMayo 1983: 381).

Table 6.1 summarizes the history of construction of the SSN 688 class nuclear attack submarine. Each submarine cost about $140 million in 1978 US dollars. Only two shipyards, Newport News and Electric Boat, were equipped to build this type of submarine. The ceiling price, the maximum amount the government was required to pay the contractor, is given as a percentage of the target or bid cost. As the third column of the table shows, the value of the cost-share parameter varied considerably during the eleven years between the awarding of the first contract and the awarding of the last contract. While there was probably considerable uncertainty associated with the first contract, costs must have become much more predictable over time. Consequently, all else being equal, the cost-share parameter should have declined over time, as the need for the government to bear some of the risk declined. While the sharing ratio was smaller in 1981 than it had been in 1970, no regular pattern of decline in the cost-share parameter is discernible in Table 6.1; indeed, between 1971 and 1975 the value of the cost-share parameter increased, even though the amount of risk associated with the project was presumably declining. (However, all else

TABLE 6.1
Cost shares in a series of US Navy shipbuilding contracts

Date	Number of ships	Cost-share parameter (α)		Ceiling price (%)	Contractor
02/70	1	0.70		125	Newport News
01/71	7	0.70		116	Electric Boat
01/71	4	0.70		111	Newport News
10/73	11	0.85	(3%)	123	Electric Boat
		0.70			
08/75	5	0.95	(11%)	133	Newport News
		0.85			
09/77	3	0.80		135	Newport News
04/79	2	0.80		135	Electric Boat
08/81	3	0.50		130	Newport News

SOURCE: De Mayo (1983: 376, 383-4)

The amount of competition varied from contract to contract. In some instances there was no bidding competition: the contract was simply negotiated with one of the two qualified firms. In other instances, the competition was extremely close. In 1979, for example, the closeness of the competition led the winner, the Electric Boat Company, to submit a lower bid than the Navy had expected. In this instance, Navy officials suspected the firms of indulging in 'gaming'—that is, in deliberately submitting a bid lower than the cost the firm actually intends to aim for, so that a cost overrun is almost certain. Recall from the theoretical analysis, however, that so long as the final payment to the firm is directly related to its bid (that is, the parameter β is strictly positive) and the cost-share parameter, α, is optimally chosen, then bidding below expected cost will not increase the price ultimately paid by the government. Even if there will, on average, be a cost overrun, the government's expected payment is minimized. The reason why deliberate underbidding does matter in practice is the government's willingness to change the terms of the contract: the firm 'buys in' to the project by submitting an unrealistically low bid; it then recoups its losses by persuading the government to renegotiate the contract because of unexpected increases in costs. According to documents released in 1984 by Senator William Proxmire, General Dynamics (which owns Electric Boat) submitted a claim against the Navy in 1976 for increased costs on the 1971 and 1973 688 submarine contracts (see Table 6.1). The company based its claim on the contention that construction of the submarines had been delayed because the Navy had supplied unsuitable blueprints and ordered design changes. However, there was evidence that delays were largely caused by Electric Boat's management problems: long drawn-out labour negotiations, understaffing, and inadequate supervision of workers. By 1977, Electric Boat was reportedly losing $15 million per month on the 688 project. To enforce its claim, the company threatened to shut down the 688 program if it were not offered substantial contract price increases. The Navy and General Dynamics then apparently co-operated on the claim. According to the minutes of a February 1978 General Dynamics board meeting, 'Representatives of the corporation are working cooperatively with civilian representatives of the Navy, including Secretary Claytor and Assistant Secretary Hidalgo, to develop a document that will present the 688 picture and financial impact the program would have on the corporation if relief is not provided. Preparation of the request has been complicated by the fact that it cannot be based on the failing-business doctrine. A great deal of hard creative work will be required to develop a convincing rationale acceptable to Congress' (*New York Times*, 23 September 1984). Ultimately, in the face of General Dynamic's threats to shut down the program, the Navy agreed to pay $634 million above the original contract price for the 18 submarines.

According to the theoretical analysis, one of the determinants of the optimal cost-share parameter in an incentive contract is the degree of the contractor's risk aversion. If firms are heavily dependent on a single line of business for survival, they are likely to exhibit some risk aversion. Military contracts generate most of the revenue of some firms. For example, in 1983, General Dynamics held nearly $6.8 billion worth of defence contracts; its annual revenue was $7.1 billion. McDonnell Douglas held over $6.1 billion in defence contracts; its annual revenue was $8.1 billion. (Comparisons of value of contracts held and annual revenue are somewhat misleading, however, since many of the contracts span several years.) The avoidance of risk is presumably a feature of these firms' behaviour. The DOD routinely allows a higher negotiated target profit to contractors who bear a higher financial risk: in other words, the government acts as though it believes the contractors are risk averse.

As Table 6.1 indicates, the incentive contracts used by the Department of Defense usually have a ceiling price as well as a target cost (bid); if costs rise enough to hit the ceiling, the contract effectively becomes a fixed-price contract. In practice, contractors often appear to be more concerned about the ceiling cost than they are about the target cost. The incentive effects of the cost-share parameter are often ignored. This may happen because the chosen sharing parameter gives too small a part of any cost overrun or cost underrun to the firm. A typical value of α under DOD incentive contracts is 0.8; that is, the contractor pays only 20 cents for each dollar of cost overrun. This amount may be too small to outweigh the contractor's benefits from inflating his costs (benefits that he will realize, for example, in his private-sector business or his future DOD business).

Empirical evidence suggests that the target cost (or bid) for incentive contracts decreases as the cost-share parameter, α, increases (that is, as the contract becomes closer to cost-plus). This outcome is in accord with the theoretical analysis in Chapter 3. It has also been found that ex ante profit rates (based on target cost rather than actual cost) decrease as α increases. This outcome too is in accord with the theory: the increase in bidding competition and the decrease in the risk borne by the firm that accompany an increase in α both result in a lower expected profit.

7. SUBCONTRACTING[2]

Although the large contractors, such as General Dynamics and McDonnell Douglas, are the most visible firms in the US military industry, these firms subcontract much of the actual work to smaller firms. Typically, 50-60 per cent of the work on a weapons system is contracted out by the prime contractor. Thus the US military industry has a two-tiered structure: an upper level of large contractors and a lower level of smaller subcontractors.

The prime contractor is faced with a 'make or buy' decision. The amount of business contracted out by a large contractor fluctuates greatly from year to year; generally it accounts for between 30 per cent and 70 per cent of the firm's total business. These fluctuations allow the large firm to smooth its output over time. When demand is high, the large firm contracts out much of its work. When demand is low, the large firm does the work itself. (The opportunity cost of the large firm's using its own labour force and machinery is lower when demand is low.) Thus, according to some observers, the large contractors shift the risk from demand fluctuations to the subcontractors.

Because the subcontractors are specialized in particular lines of business, they frequently have lower production costs than the prime contractors. However, because the Department of Defense's common use of cost-plus contracts gives the prime contractor no incentive to hold its own costs down, the prime contractor often chooses to do the work in-house when it would be less costly to have a subcontractor do it.

Although the subcontractors face more risk than the large contractors, there is evidence that subcontractors' profits are significantly lower than large contractors' profits. There appears to be more price competition at the subcontractors' level than there is at the prime contractors' level.

The issues that face a government in deciding how to write a contract with a firm (as discussed in Chapter 3) have their equivalent in the issues that face a prime contractor in deciding what kind of contract to offer to a subcontractor. One study of DOD contracts found that in 85 per cent of the cases in which the prime contractor had a cost-plus contract the subcontractors were working under fixed-price contracts (including some research and development subcontracts) (Gansler 1980).

---

2   The information in this section is drawn from Gansler (1980: chap. 6).

8. SUMMARY

This chapter has had two purposes: to illustrate some of the problems that arise in government/firm contracting and to show that incentive contracts, so far from being just some theoretical abstraction, have been used successfully by a large government agency.

It should be stressed, however, that it is not our purpose to advocate that other government agencies merely imitate the US Department of Defense's use of incentive contracts. To the contrary, this chapter has sought to demonstrate the problems associated with the DOD's practice of choosing the cost-share parameter arbitrarily. The theory in Chapter 3 showed that the optimal cost-share parameter depends on several underlying parameters of the individual contracting situation. The simulations in Chapters 4 and 5 illustrated the practical implementation of the theory. The systematic procedure advocated by this study is designed to approximate, as closely as possible, the theoretically ideal contract.

7

Ontario Contracting Rules

This chapter describes the Ontario government's rules covering contracting procedures.[1] Some of these rules are given in the *Ontario Manual of Administration*, which binds government ministries but not the provincial Crown corporations.[2]

1. TENDERING CONTRACTS

The government agency either advertises for bids in the newspapers or invites particular firms to submit bids. In the latter case, the invited firms are drawn from a list maintained by the government agency. This list is required to be open-ended, so that extra firms can be added to it at any time. The agency makes a choice between using a public tender and inviting specific firms to bid in accordance with its own internal purchasing procedures. When the agency does not hold a public tender, it must request bids from at least three firms. If the agency requests or receives fewer than three bids, it must document the reasons.

One or two examples of how specific agencies use these procedures are in order. The Ministry of Government Services usually advertises projects by public tender. Occasionally, however, it decides to call tenders by invitation. For this purpose, the ministry keeps a list of contractors' names, from which it chooses the bidders—there are usually six—on a rotating basis. Similarly, the Ministry of Transportation and Communications advertises all tenders except those for very specialized equipment, such as electronic weigh-scales or

1 We are grateful to Mr R. Armstrong of the Ministry of Natural Resources, Ms V. Gibbons of the Management Board of Cabinet, Mr J. Kryzanowski of Ontario Hydro, Mr D.E. Thrasher of the Ministry of Transportation and Communications, and Mr A.W. Thurston of the Ministry of Government Services for supplying us with information on contracting procedures.
2 The Organization for Economic Co-operation and Development (1976b) has published a summary of all its members' government-procurement procedures. The reader interested in other countries' procurement policies should consult this book.

electronic traffic management systems, which can be supplied by only a small number of firms. In such cases, the ministry invites bids from a list of qualified suppliers.

Before the government agency requests bids, it must develop objective criteria for choosing the successful bidder. The bidding firms must be informed what these selection criteria are. A bid is to be judged responsible if it meets pre-established criteria for determining whether the firm would be capable of carrying out the contract. These criteria might include a particular kind of expertise, a demonstrated ability to meet target dates, and a given degree of previous experience.

The envelopes containing the bids may not be opened until the designated time. The bids are opened in public. The name and address of the bidder and the amount bid are announced. Normally, the firm that submits the lowest responsible bid is selected. If the lowest bid is not selected, the government agency must document its reasons for rejecting the bid.

The Ministry of Transportation and Communications requires each bidder to submit a deposit with the bid. The ministry returns the deposits after the tenders are opened; however, the winning bidder's deposit is forfeit if he fails to enter into a contract after being notified of his bid's success.

The Ministry of Transportation and Communications requires the contractor to sign a statement to the effect that 'The Bidder expressly warrants that the prices contained in his tender whether as unit prices or lump sums, and whether for transportation or supply of materials or for services, are quoted in utmost good faith on his part, without any collusive arrangement or agreement with any other person, or partnership or corporation. The Bidder expressly represents that he is not party or privy to any deceit tending to mislead the Ministry into accepting his tenders as a truly competitive tender whether to the prejudice, injury or benefit of the Ministry.'

For certain professional consulting services, the agency does not have to select the lowest responsible bid. Cost is only one of several selection criteria; the others can include qualifications or expertise, previous experience and performance, availability, previous share of ministry business, ability to deliver, knowledge of local standards, proximity to the work site, understanding of objectives, quality of the proposed approach, and any other criteria that the agency considers appropriate. A project whose estimated cost is less than $15,000 need not be tendered.

For technical consulting services (architects, accountants, engineers, scientists, etc.), the government agency may, according to the circumstances, use either competitive or non-competitive selection procedures. The competitive selection procedures apply if the assignment is non-routine and investigative, or if the fees for the required technical services vary among suppliers. The agency may use the non-competitive selection procedures if the assignment is a clearly defined one 'consisting mainly of the routine application of standard technical methods leading to a predetermined end result' and if the fees for the required technical services do not vary significantly among suppliers. The agency may also use non-competitive selection procedures if, in the opinion of the deputy minister, the competitive selection procedure would result in unacceptable delays in completing the project. If the agency follows the competitive selection procedure, it solicits detailed proposals from at least three and, normally, not more than six qualified suppliers. The proposals must contain the following: an outline of the work to be done; a timetable for the completion of each stage of the project; the names, qualifications, and experience of the staff to be assigned to the project; per diem rates for each person involved; and an estimated total cost, with a ceiling price if possible. If the agency uses the non-competitive selection procedures, its selection committee must nominate at least three qualified suppliers, rank them according to various relevant criteria, and forward its recommendations to the deputy minister, who makes a selection 'with a view to achieving an equitable distribution of Ministry assignments among qualified suppliers.' The selection committee then negotiates an agreement with the selected firm.

For any research and development project, the rules require the government agency to compare the costs and benefits of contracting the work out with those of doing it in-house. The agency must contract out the research and development work unless there is a clear case for the agency's doing it itself.

Competitive proposals are not required for research and development assignments with an estimated total cost of less than $15,000. For a project expected to cost more than $15,000, the selection procedure is to send the project specifications and a request for letters of qualification to possible contractors. On the basis of the letters of qualification, the agency invites at least three potential contractors to submit proposals. The agency must document its reasons for the selection of the successful contractor. The agency may accept unsolicited research proposals if the area of research is consistent with its objectives and if the government's interests would not be better served by calling for competitive proposals on the project.

Contracts for advertising and public relations services (or, as the *Ontario Manual of Administration* calls them, in something approaching Orwellian Newspeak, 'creative communication services') are awarded competitively. The competitive process consists of inviting not fewer than three and not more than five advertising agencies to give presentations of their work before ministry representatives. The criteria for selection include knowledge of the objectives and the needs of the ministry, knowledge of the communications market, evidence of a sufficiently high standard of creativity, past performance and professional qualifications of the personnel, and such less objective criteria as what the regulations call 'personal chemistry.' Price does not appear to be one of the officially required criteria.

Ontario Hydro's regulations state that 'Ontario Hydro will purchase without favouritism at the lowest overall long-term cost taking into consideration vendor capability, the application of procurement strategy, and all relevant factors over the life cycle of the requirement.' Also, 'Ontario Hydro will allow any person or enterprise in Canada capable of supplying a satisfactory product or service the opportunity of bidding on the Corporation's requirements and in this regard the Corporation will not specify its requirements so as to restrict competition.' Ontario Hydro may waive requirement for competitive tendering in certain circumstances: when there is only a single vendor capable of supplying the product or service (for example, proprietary spare parts); in order to save time in emergency situations; where prices are regulated so that competition could not affect the price; and in hiring consultants if the consultants have demonstrated their abilities in past work for Ontario Hydro. With a few specific exceptions, tenders for construction and for service requirements are publicly advertised. Tenders for material are solicited by private invitation from suppliers of demonstrated capability. Proposals for consultant services are also solicited by private invitation. Publicly advertised tenders are opened in public. Privately solicited tenders are opened in private: the policy is not to let the firms know how many other firms have been approached, or the identities of the other firms. The contract is awarded to 'the bidder evaluated as offering the lowest cost and who is capable of supplying the required material or services within the required time frame.'[3]

2. DOMESTIC PREFERENCES

In order to encourage 'Canadian firms to compete for government business against foreign producers of goods and services,' the Ontario government has a Canadian preference policy. The bidding firms are asked to state the amount of Canadian content contained in their bids. Canadian content is defined as 'the difference between the laid-down cost and the dutiable value of imported goods or imported parts. Thus all values added in Canada, including labour, materials, transportation, duty and taxes, and the Canadian suppliers' profit fall into Canadian content.' The government agency then allows a price preference of 10 per cent on Canadian content. For example, if a bid with 100 per cent foreign content is no more than 5 per cent lower than a bid with 50 per cent foreign content and 50 per cent Canadian content, the higher bid will be accepted. (Table 9.1 in Chapter 9 provides some actual instances of such computations.) The contract form of the Ministry of Government Services states that 'all material, plant and equipment supplied for the work shall have the maximum possible Canadian content.' For advertising services, Ontario government agencies may consider only wholly Canadian-owned companies.

Ontario Hydro has a more stringent domestic preference policy than the

---

3 The foregoing description of bidding rules is drawn from the following: *Ontario Manual of Administration*, pp. 35-4-1 to 35-4-6, pp. 50-3-1 to 50-3-5, pp. 50-4-1 to 50-4-7, and pp. 50-9-3 to 59-9-6; Ontario Ministry of Transportation and Communications (1977, 1983); Ontario Management Board of Cabinet (1983); and Ontario Hydro (1981-84, pp. SP2-1-3 to SP2-1-8, SP3-5-1 to SP3-5-8, and SP3-7-1 to SP-7-4).

Ontario ministries. It offers a 10 per cent price preference for Canadian content, or 15 per cent when a foreign bidder receives subsidized financing. It accepts bids from foreign firms only if two Canadian bidders cannot be found. Where possible, it splits projects into two or more contracts, in order to increase the opportunities for Canadian firms to compete with foreign firms. It offers a 3 per cent price preference for Ontario content over non-Ontario Canadian content.

Although Ontario universities are not bound by the Canadian preference policy of the Ontario government, a joint working group of the Council of Ontario Universities and the Ministry of Industry and Trade has produced a set of guidelines that favours Canadian companies. They apply to purchases of over $10,000, although certain commodities are exempt. Like the Ontario government ministries, the universities give a price preference of 10 per cent on the basis of Canadian content. Individual universities decide for themselves whether to follow the guidelines.

In 1981, the Office of Procurement Policy was instituted as a part of the Ministry of Industry and Trade to administer the Canadian preference policy and to work towards increasing the Canadian contents of the goods and services purchased by provincial government agencies. It seeks to encourage Canadian firms to bid on government contracts by supplying them with information about opportunities to do business with public bodies and about tendering procedures. It also monitors individual ministries' compliance with the Canadian preference policy. It has the right to recommend to Cabinet that preferences of more than 10 per cent be offered in particular circumstances.[4]

3. TYPES OF CONTRACT

The general policy of the Ontario government with respect to price quotations is as follows: 'Only firm prices shall be solicited from potential suppliers. Ministries shall not include terms permitting price escalation in bid documents or in contracts. Ministries shall not reopen contracts to take into account increased costs where the other terms and conditions of supply remain unchanged. Failure of suppliers to meet the terms of contracts shall be dealt with by means other than the renegotiation of prices.'

The Ministry of Transportation and Communications usually offers fixed-price contracts. However, the price can be renegotiated either up or down if the project's specifications are changed after the contract has been signed. If, during the course of the work, the contractor finds some way of changing the specifications of the project that will lower its total costs, then the contract may be renegotiated. The firm's incentive to discover cost-reducing changes in the project's design is that it shares in the resultant savings, usually on a fifty-fifty basis. Significant savings have been achieved in this way in urban freeway

---

4   On the Ontario domestic preference policy, see Ontario Ministry of Industry and Trade (1983).

construction. (Note, however, that this arrangement is not an incentive contract: it is a fixed-price contract with a provision for renegotiation of the fixed price if the project's specifications are changed.)

The Ministry of Transportation and Communications uses cost-plus (or 'force-account') contracts 'where it is impractical to negotiate a price or where agreement cannot be reached on a price for approved extra work.' Work performed on a cost-plus basis is supervised by a ministry official, who keeps daily work records reporting the amount of labour, materials, and equipment used; each day's record must be signed by a representative of the contractor.

The Ministry of Government Services uses fixed-price (or 'lump-sum') contracts for most purposes. An exception to this rule is the occasional project for which the construction-management approach is appropriate. The construction-management approach involves hiring a construction manager, usually at the design stage of a project, to advise on construction techniques, costs, and the availability of labour and materials. The ministry uses this method in three kinds of situations: when the project is complex, where tight scheduling is necessary, and when the project is not fully defined at the outset and its specifications will be modified during the course of construction. The advantage of the construction-management method is its flexibility: rather than having to await the completion of the project's drawings and specifications and then offer a single fixed-price tender, the ministry can offer a sequence of smaller contract packages as the project proceeds. The companies that undertake construction management include both general construction contractors and specialized construction-management companies. The ministry maintains a list of construction managers. For any particular project, some firms chosen from this list are asked for quotations on a fee and salary basis. The ministry then selects one firm to manage the project, which proceeds on a cost-plus basis.

For professional consulting services, the Ontario ministries use cost-plus contracts. More specifically, the contract specifies the per diem rate to be charged for each individual working on the project, but the number of days to be worked is not specified and therefore neither is the final total cost. If there are published fee schedules established by recognized professional associations, the per diem rates are normally set in accordance with these schedules. The contract states an estimated total cost and, where possible, a ceiling price as well.

Before a government agency contracts for technical consulting services or management consulting services, it must ensure that the assignment is properly defined. This means that 'the requirements of the assignment' must be 'documented and clearly understood' and that 'the supplier's output can be measured against defined objectives.'

Contracts for advertising and public relations services are awarded either for a single project (on a cost-plus basis) or by an agency agreement, which is a long-term contract (up to three years in duration) to provide some or all of the advertising and public-relations services required by a ministry. During the term of an agency agreement, the ministry may commission projects without further competitive selection. The performance of an advertising agency under a multi-year contract is reviewed annually. The goals and measurement criteria for projects are written into the contract. The cost-plus contract works as follows: the agency charges the ministry on a fee-for-service hourly basis when it is invited by the ministry to discuss new projects; consultation fees for assigned projects are written into the project budget; the agency charges the ministry cost plus a fixed percentage of cost to cover the expenses of placing advertisements in any communications medium; transportation and other expenses are covered by the ministry.

As we noted in Chapters 2 and 3, contract performance will improve (from the point of view of both the government and the firm) if some sources of uncertainty can be eliminated. That inflation is a removable source of uncertainty is taken into account by Ontario Hydro's regulations: 'In recognition of the uncertainties concerning trends in the costs of labour and materials in long-term contracts ... Ontario Hydro will enter into a contract with prices subject to escalation provided that the value of the contract exceeds $200,000 and delivery extends beyond one year from date of tender.' The price escalation is based on an official Statistics Canada industry price index. Also, payments for contracts that have a significant import component, and that are therefore affected by fluctuations in the exchange rate, may be adjusted in accordance with the exchange rate.

If Ontario Hydro judges that it is put at risk because a prospective supplier is in a doubtful financial condition, it may require the firm to post a performance bond.[5]

4. CONTRACT PROVISIONS

The decision to audit cost claims on a cost-plus contract is made by the individual ministry. Any claim about which there are questions is likely to be audited.

Both the Ministry of Government Services and the Ministry of Transportation and Communications give contractors a pecuniary incentive to complete the work on time. This is done by paying each month 90 per cent of the value of the work so far completed (this value computed proportionately to the total value of the contract). The balance owing under the contract is paid when the project is complete and the ministry has judged that the quality of the work conforms to the terms of the contract.

Although the contracts for construction awarded by the Ministry of

5 The rules governing contract form are described in the following: *Ontario Manual of Administration*, pp. 35-7-1 to 35-7-4, pp. 50-3-1 to 50-3-5, and pp. 50-4-1 to 50-4-7; Ontario Ministry of Transportation and Communications (1982a); Ontario Ministry of Government Services (1983); Ontario Management Board of Cabinet (1983); and Ontario Hydro (1981-84, pp. SP3-106-1 to SP3-106-3 and SP3-7-2). The federal government's rules about professional consulting contracts are similar; see Treasury Board of Canada (1980).

Government Services are usually fixed-price contracts, they are written in such a way that some risk is borne by the government. The specifications of the project describe the soil conditions at the work site. If the actual soil conditions differ significantly from the description, and if the contractor demonstrates that he had incurred unforeseen extra costs as a result of this difference, then the ministry will make an extra payment to compensate for these costs. Conversely, if the ministry judges that a difference in soil conditions results in a saving in the contractor's costs, it can reduce its payment to the firm.

At any stage in the course of a project, the Ministry of Government Services may inspect the work. Any work judged by the ministry not to conform with the contract must be replaced at the contractor's expense. If the ministry decides that it is not expedient to replace the work, it deducts from its contracted payment to the firm an amount equal to the difference between the value of the work defined in the contract and the value of the defective work. The ministry's ultimate sanction against work of poor quality is termination of the contract. It can take this step if the contractor neglects to pursue the work diligently or uses substandard materials or insufficiently skilled workers. After termination, the work is completed by whatever means the ministry deems expedient, at the contractor's expense. The Ministry of Transportation and Communications has similar termination procedures.

The contracts issued by the Ministry of Transportation and Communications contain liquidated damage clauses. If the project is not completed on time, the contractor pays the government a specified sum for each day's delay. The amount of money to be paid is written into the contract: it is an estimate of the actual loss or damage to the ministry resulting from the delay.

The Ministry of Transportation and Communications has a system of qualification procedures designed to ensure that any firm that submits bids is financially and technically capable of performing the work. Once a year, potential contractors submit to the ministry financial statements, statements of their relevant experience, and descriptions of the equipment owned by their firms. On the basis of this information, the ministry gives each firm a rating. This basic rating is a numerical summary of the information. The basic rating may be adjusted after the firm has completed work for the ministry. If the quality of the firm's work is unsatisfactory, the ministry lowers its rating; the amount of the reduction depends on how poor the work was, the extent of the contractor's responsibility for the poor quality of the work, and the frequency of work of poor quality. When a project is advertised for tender, the advertisement includes a statement of the minimum rating a firm must have in order to be allowed to submit a bid. In this way, the firm is given a direct incentive not to do work of poor quality: poor work lowers the firm's chances of receiving a contract from the ministry in the future.

When a firm under contract to supply technical consulting services completes an assignment, the government agency must prepare an evaluation of the firm's performance. The evaluation is retained for three years, and other government agencies have access to it. This measure may provide firms with some incentive to avoid work of poor quality (Ontario Ministry of Transportation and Communications 1982a, b; Ontario 1976-83).

In 1977, the Ontario legislature passed new audit legislation defining the role of the provincial auditor in the government's financial control process. The provincial auditor annually tables in the legislature a report on a wide range of financial matters. Part of the power of the provincial auditor comes from the publicity that follows the publication of his annual report, in which he can exercise considerable discretion in choosing which matters to single out for comment. The report assesses the 'economy, efficiency, and effectiveness' of a government agency's programs: it addresses such questions as whether a particular activity needed as much money as was actually spent on it, whether the inputs used in an activity were justified by the resulting outputs, and whether the government agency had adequate procedures for evaluating the extent of a program's success. In addition to preparing his annual report, the provincial auditor is required to audit the financial statements of government agencies. A further function of the provincial auditor is to investigate specific matters at the request of the legislature or the cabinet. The provincial auditor is empowered to examine individuals under oath about matters related to such special investigations. At the invitation of the legislature's Public Accounts Committee, the provincial auditor may attend the committee's meetings in order to provide assistance to the committee. There is a Board of Internal Economy, a committee of the Ontario legislative assembly, to audit the provincial auditor.[6]

Contractors are required to pay any sales taxes imposed on the inputs they use in government projects. The Retail Sales Tax Act regards the firm as the consumer of any equipment or supplies acquired in the ordinary course of its business. Thus the tax payable by the contractor must be included in the contract price (Ontario Ministry of Transportation and Communications 1982a; Ontario Ministry of Government Services 1983).

---

6 On the audit legislation of the Ontario government and the functions of the provincial auditor, see Denham (1978).

8

Ontario Contracting Practices

The sums paid to private firms by Ontario government agencies are very large: in 1981-82 private firms received a total of $9 billion from the provincial government, provincial crown corporations, municipal governments, and the public health and education agencies. The biggest spenders among the government ministries are the Ministry of Government Services, which provides centralized purchasing for the Ontario government agencies of accommodation facilities and other goods and services and spends about $45 million annually on supplies and equipment and about $160 million on services; the Ministry of Transportation and Communications, whose annual purchases of $102 million worth of supplies and equipment and $92 million worth of services are used mainly on construction and maintenance of highways; and the Ministry of Natural Resources, whose annual expenditure of $54 million for supplies and equipment and $100 million for services goes to outdoor recreation facilities, resource development, and the conservation of public lands. Ontario hospitals spend over $700 million on goods and services each year, and the publicly funded education sector's annual expenditure on goods and services is more than $1 billion. At the end of 1983 a single crown corporation, Ontario Hydro, had $2.1 billion in outstanding commitments for equipment, materials, and services.[1]

This chapter applies the theoretical analysis developed earlier to the Ontario government's experience with contracting, pinpointing some of the pitfalls associated with government/firm contracts.

1. BIDDING COMPETITION

The rules laid down by the Ontario government in the *Ontario Manual of Administration* require its agencies to select contractors by inviting sealed-bid

---

1 Ontario Ministry of Industry and Trade (1983); Ontario Hydro (1983). The figures apply to 1981-82 unless otherwise stated. For more details on spending by Ontario government agencies, see Ontario Ministry of Treasury and Economics (1983a, b, c).

tenders and choosing the lowest responsible bid. The process is open in the sense that, on the specified day, the bids are opened in public and the bids are announced. The theoretical analysis presented earlier supports this arrangement as being the appropriate way of selecting the contractor. There are three advantages to sealed-bid tenders. First, provided that the final amount paid to the firm is related to its bid, the lowest bidder will be the firm with the lowest expected costs for the particular project. Second, the public opening of tenders makes it difficult for firms and government officials to carry out any under-the-table deals. Third, the use of sealed-bid tenders generates lower bids than do other tendering mechanisms, such as having an auctioneer call bids openly. In view of these advantages, we support the existing Ontario tendering process and recommend that no change be made in it.

The appropriate tendering procedures are not always followed. Some observers claim that cabinet ministers and senior bureaucrats use the awarding of contracts as a form of patronage. Thus the chairman of Ontario Parliament's Public Accounts Committee has cited cases of improper contracting by the Ministry of Industry and Trade, the Ministry of Agriculture and Food, the Ministry of Citizenship and Culture, the Ministry of Government Services, and the Ministry of Tourism and Recreation. Contracts with values up to $600,000 were awarded untendered, in breach of the Ontario government's rules (*London Free Press*, 1 March 1984).

In 1982-83, the Ministry of Government Services awarded untendered eight successive contracts to Allan W. Foster and Associates Limited for the development and implementation of a manpower planning system for the ministry. Each of the eight contracts was worth less than $15,000, but their total value was $81,300. The purpose of this division of the project into many small contracts appears to have been to circumvent the *Ontario Manual of Administration*, which requires tendering for management consulting contracts worth more than $15,000 (Ontario 1983).

The provincial auditor's *Annual Report* for 1983 cited irregularities in the hiring of consultants by the Ontario Waste Management Corporation. The corporation retained a consulting firm for $31,000 to prepare job descriptions for the corporation's employees. The provincial auditor found that 'no competitive bids were obtained from other suppliers. We understood that the consulting firm was recommended by a member of the Corporation's Board of Directors.' Another consulting firm was engaged for $110,000 to 'establish the rationale for facilities system selection.' The provincial auditor noted that 'the firm was hired without obtaining competitive bids from other suppliers. We understood that this firm was recommended by one of the Corporation's employees.' The provincial auditor also noted three other instances in which this corporation offered contracts without inviting tenders (Provincial Auditor of Ontario 1983: 156-7).

The cases cited here are of interest not just because rules were broken, but because of the practical effects of this rule-breaking. In each of these cases, there was no bidding competition. An absence of bidding competition tends, for two reasons, to raise the cost of a contract to the government. First, since only one firm bids, there is no guarantee that the lowest-cost firm receives the contract; competitive bidding reveals the firms' relative expected costs. Second, even if the lowest-cost firm is chosen, there is no downward pressure on the price the firm negotiates with the government, as there would be if the firm faced competition for the job. Thus, as was shown in Chapter 4, an absence of bidding competition can substantially raise the price to the government of a project.

It is the role of the Management Board of the cabinet, the Public Accounts Committee, and the provincial auditor to detect improper tendering procedures. We shall not discuss this question in the present study.

As a rule, tenders are publicly advertised. Occasionally, however, government agencies invite bids from a few selected firms. The long-term relationship between the government agency and particular firms that develops through the latter procedure has both its benefits and its costs.

The benefits are that the government officials know which firms are capable of undertaking particular tasks and which are likely to be the least expensive. A firm that is on a list of potential invitees has an incentive not to do inferior work: work of poor quality might result in the firm's being struck off the list and losing its opportunities for future profitable government contracts.

The major cost of the procedure of inviting firms to bid is that the government officials might unconsciously start acting in the interests of the firms. This idea is similar to George Stigler's theory of economic regulation: 'As a rule, regulation is acquired by the industry and is designed and operated primarily for its benefit' (Stigler 1975: 114). In other words, the regulatory body tends to be captured by, and to become the instrument of, the regulated firms, reversing the putative order of things. For example, an air transport regulatory body will typically make decisions that benefit the airlines rather than consumers. Stigler further noted that one of the major public resources 'commonly sought by an industry is control over entry by new rivals' (ibid., 116). If the firms can use the regulatory body to restrict entry, they can earn large profits without having to worry that the profits will attract new entrants to the industry who will compete the profits away. A similar potential for misdirected decisions may be present when a government agency regularly awards contracts to the same small group of firms: it may confuse the interests of these firms with the interests of the public. The firms may be able to abuse the trust they have built up with government officials by doing good work in the past.

For this reason, the Ontario government is to be commended for having set up the Office of Procurement Policy. While the primary purpose of this body is to administer a government policy of giving preference to Canadian firms, it has a secondary purpose of encouraging Canadian firms not normally engaged in government business to seek government contracts. The fact that the office is a separate agency that does not offer contracts itself reduces the likelihood that it will fall into the trap of fostering the interests of a particular industry. Because the office does not deal with a single group of firms, it can take an overall view of contracting questions.

As we suggested in Chapter 4, one way of increasing the number of bidders is to split projects into subprojects. Ontario Hydro takes this idea one step further by allowing the bidding firms themselves to suggest how to split a project: a firm can submit a bid that is conditional on the project's being split in a particular way. Thus Ontario Hydro uses the firms' knowledge to find the natural points at which projects can be split; these natural splits might be based, for example, on technical grounds or on volume grounds.

When a project is being repeated, the government can achieve some economies by having the same firm do the job each time: designs do not have to be redrawn, specialized skills do not have to be relearned, and existing tooling can be reused. Opportunities for such economies occur, for example, when the project is the duplication of a large nuclear or fossil-fuelled power station. The disadvantage of using the same firm is that, after the first project has been completed, the firm is in a sole-source position: it could use its monopoly power to drive up the price.

Ontario Hydro has a policy designed to secure the advantages of duplication without the disadvantages. This policy makes use of the fact that if the project was tendered competitively the first time the bidding competition would have kept the price down, giving Ontario Hydro some idea of the true costs of the project. The supplier therefore runs the risk of losing the contract if during the negotiations for the second project he asks an unduly high price. Hydro expects that the asking price for the second project will be lower than the price for the first project, reflecting the economies from duplication. However, it also recognizes that general inflation may have raised prices between the awarding of the first contract and the negotiations for the second contract (Ontario Hydro 1977).

According to the theoretical analysis, competition in bidding will drive down the expected price paid by the government as long as the bidders have different expected costs. Only if all bidders have the same expected costs is bidding competition inconsequential. According to the theory, a firm will bid the higher the higher are its expected costs: thus the fact that for any actual project there is almost always a range of bids is evidence that firms usually do have different expected costs, and that therefore competition in bidding matters. An apparent exception to this rule occurs when the firms in question provide technical consulting services for which the fees are set by a professional association. Since the relevant firms will all have the same accounting costs, the *Ontario Manual of Administration* recommends that government agencies use non-competitive selection procedures in such cases.

It is an error, however, to conclude that the theory justifies using non-competitive selection procedures when consultants' fees are identical. As we explained in Chapter 2, the relevant costs are not accounting costs, but economic costs. One of the factors that determines how low a firm will bid is the extent of the firm's alternative opportunities. Even if all firms have the same accounting costs, because fees are set by a professional association, they will usually not have the same economic costs: the firms will differ in their opportunity costs because they have different alternative opportunities in their private-sector and other public-sector business. Thus there remains a role for competitive bidding, which will reveal the firm with the lowest opportunity cost; that is, the firm that is willing to do the work for the lowest price. (As we noted earlier, however, if the contract is cost-plus, as technical consulting contracts usually are, then the contractor's ultimate profit is not related to the costs he incurs; consequently competitive bidding does not reveal which firm has the lowest economic costs. Given a cost-plus contract, non-competitive selection procedures are no worse than competitive selection procedures. But, as argued before, the cost-plus contract cannot be the optimal contract.)

Ontario Hydro has developed a clever and simple way of dealing with the problem of few bidders. Hydro's policy is to keep the number of bidders secret. The firms will base their bids on the number of bidders they expect to participate. Thus if there are fewer bidders than the firms expect, their bids will be lower than they ought to be. By the same token, if there are more bidders than the firms expect, their bids will be higher than they ought to be. Ontario Hydro derives its advantage from the fact that increasing the number of bidders brings diminishing returns to the principal. The advantage to the principal of there being extra bidders is reduced when the number of bidders is high. Thus the savings to the principal from the firms' bidding as if there were more bidders than there are exceed the costs to the principal of the firms' bidding as if there were fewer bidders than there are. This policy is recommended when there are often very few bidders and the bidders are risk averse. (We develop this argument in detail in McAfee and McMillan [1987a].)

The greater is the number of firms submitting bids, the greater is the bidding competition and therefore the lower is the expected cost of the project for the government. Again, however, there is a diminishing-returns effect: the greater is the number of bidders, the smaller is the effect of one extra bidder on the government's expected payment. One realistic aspect of the bidding situation not included in the theoretical model is the fact that evaluating bids is a costly process for the government agency, especially if the bidding is for technical consulting services, in which case the capability of each bidder must be evaluated in several dimensions, or for projects where competition is over design as well as price. Thus there is an optimal number of bids, a number that represents a balance between the benefits of increased bidding competition (which reduces the government's expected payment) and the costs of evaluating extra bids. (We address this question in McAfee and McMillan [1987b].)

2. COLLUSION IN BIDDING

The theory developed in Chapter 3 assumed that the bidders behave non-cooperatively: there is no collusion among the bidders. The theory applies even when collusion does exist—but then the outcome is as if there were only one bidder, rather than the several bidders ostensibly present. That is, collusion eliminates the bidding-competition effect.

How much collusion occurs in the Ontario context is not an easy question to answer. To the extent that collusion is successful, it is, by definition, not observed by anyone outside the industry. Collusion is observed only when it breaks down. Nevertheless, collusion does not appear to be a serious problem in Ontario government/firm contracting.

However, examples of collusion do exist.[2] Firms that produce metal culverts for drainage have a long history of price fixing. The main purchasers of culverts are municipal, provincial, and federal governments. In 1974 the Supreme Court of Ontario convicted ten metal-culvert firms of price-fixing and fined them a total of over a half-million dollars. The firms had formed an association, the Canadian Steel Pipe Institute, ostensibly to encourage the use of metal rather than concrete pipe, but really to raise prices by eliminating competition. The firms co-ordinated their prices by following an open pricing policy. Each firm printed its price list and made it available to all of its customers and competitors. This measure was intended to equalize prices across firms; because price competition was eliminated, the prices were equalized at high levels. As a result, a number of the firms submitted identical bids on tenders to the Department of Highways of Ontario and to Ontario municipalities, although previously their bids had been dispersed. Remarkable precision was achieved: in one sealed-bid tender to a local government, all nine bids were for $6,009.15. It is noteworthy that it was not the conviction for price-fixing that ended the collusion. In 1967, seven years before the conviction, a new supplier of metal culverts refused to conform to the collusive pricing policy. As a result, competition among the firms resumed. This example illustrates the general proposition that cartels tend to be destroyed by their own success: the high profits from collusion attract new entrants to the industry and the profits are competed away.[3]

A second instance of collusion in government/firm contracting occurred in Windsor, Ontario, in 1963-64. Four ready-mixed concrete firms published identical price lists and agreed not to offer discounts. As a result, the firms made identical bids in municipal tenders. The first breakdown of the collusion occurred when, in a City of Windsor tender, one firm offered the city an extended payment term, contrary to the collusive agreement. When the local newspaper reported that, although all of the bids were identical, the city had accepted this firm's bid because of its extended payment term, the firm's collaborators became aware of its departure from the collusive agreement. This example illustrates a second common source of cartel breakdown: each participant in a cartel has a short-run incentive to undercut the agreed-upon

2 The following information comes from Green (1980: 109-13)
3 For a discussion of the role of new entrants in dismantling collusion, see McMillan (1986).

collusive price. In the case of the Windsor concrete firms, the one firm's cheating did not in fact destroy the price-fixing arrangement. The collusion was finally eliminated when in 1966 the four firms were found guilty of price-fixing by the Supreme Court of Ontario.

Identical bids should warn the government that the firms may be acting in collusion. (Identical bids are not definite evidence of collusion, however: according to the theory developed in Chapters 3 and 4, in the unlikely event that all of the firms have identical expected costs, they will all submit the same bid.) However, collusion may also take forms that are more difficult for the government to detect. For example, firms may arrange to take turns being the low bidder. The firms decide in advance which of them will win any particular contract; the other firms then submit higher bids in order to maintain the illusion that bidding competition exists. The low bidder bids high enough to give himself a generous profit.

The classic example of such a cartel strategy is the electrical-equipment manufacturers' conspiracy in the United States in the 1950s. The firms derived a large proportion of their sales from sealed-bid tenders to publicly owned electrical utilities. One of their schemes for rotating the winning of contracts while maintaining the appearance of competition was based on the phases of the moon. A given phase of the moon was the signal that it was a particular firm's turn to be the low bidder. That firm computed its bid by subtracting a fixed percentage from a list price previously determined by the cartel members. The remaining firms deliberately submitted higher bids. This price-fixing conspiracy was broken up by the Antitrust Division of the Justice Department in 1959. Fines were imposed on the participating firms, and some of the firms' executives went to jail.

Colluding industries sometimes switch from identical bids to rotating-bid strategies if the persistence of identical bidding has aroused the suspicion of the government purchasers. The following extract from a letter written by an executive of one firm to an executive of another firm was quoted in a 1953 Department of Justice study of identical bidding in the Canadian electrical wire and cable products industry: 'It has been suggested by our friends that in view of the fact that the Purchase Board in Ottawa may become too inquisitive in respect to agreed prices being quoted for the Department of National Defence, prices should be staggered. In other words, the business should be allocated' (quoted in Mund 1960: 162).

The electrical-equipment conspiracy shows that there is one drawback to the open tendering system (to be weighed against its previously mentioned advantages). The public opening of bids with full disclosure of each bidder's price and specifications means that cartel members quickly learn of any attempt by a firm to undercut the cartel price. They can then retaliate against the price-cutter, perhaps by starting a price war in some related market. This threat of retaliation might be enough to deter any potential price-cutter from actually going ahead with a price cut. The threat of retaliation, therefore, might make it retaliation might be enough to deter any potential price-cutter ·from actually going ahead with a price cut. The threat of retaliation, therefore, might make it possible for the cartel to persist. It is the open tendering system that makes such threats viable: obviously the cartel members could not retaliate against price cutting if they could not observe it.[4]

Again, the effect of collusion is to eliminate bidding competition. Table 4.1 provided some indication of the quantitative importance of the absence of bidding competition: using data from US military contracts, the table compared the costs of projects that had been let with bidding competition and the costs of identical projects that had been let without competition. The contracts let without bidding competition cost the government twice as much on average as the contracts let with bidding competition.

3. INCENTIVES FOR COST CONTROL

Politicians, editorial writers, and others often express alarm about the size and frequency of cost overruns in government projects. One of the lessons from the theoretical analysis of this study is that such alarm may be misplaced: persistent cost overruns do not necessarily imply mismanagement by the government. Efficient contract management by the government would ensure that the total payment by the government to the contractor is minimized. The size of a cost overrun is not, in itself, of any significance; what matters is the total cost to the government. The theory developed in Chapter 3 showed that cost overruns can occur repeatedly, and yet the government can be minimizing its expenditures.

Nevertheless, cost overruns often do indicate a failure to minimize expenditure. Thus cost overruns under cost-plus contracts are symptomatic of the fact that a cost-plus contract provides no incentive for the contractor to exert effort to keep costs low or refrain from artificially inflating his costs.

We have already mentioned cost overruns for US military contracts. Canada has its own example of escalating costs for a military contract. In 1953 Avro was awarded a $27 million contract to build two prototypes of the Arrow, a fighter airplane. In 1959, with five planes completed and six more on the production line, the project was scrapped; $450 million had been spent (*London Free Press*, 27 February 1984). Cost overruns are not confined to military contracts. Ontario Hydro's construction of nuclear generating plants was, in its early stages, especially subject to cost overruns. For example, Plant B of the Bruce Heavy Water Plant was projected, in 1973, to cost $285 million. Its actual

---

4   On rotating-bid strategies by cartels, see Comanor and Schankerman (1976). On the electrical-equipment conspiracy, see Koch (1980: 423-4). On the use of retaliatory strategies by firms to maintain collusion as an equilibrium, see McMillan (1984, 1986). However, if the firms cannot observe the others' actions, collusion may break down (Stigler 1964; Porter 1983; Robson and McMillan 1984). For more on the techniques of collusive bidding and government policies to counter collusion, see the Organization for Economic Co-operation and Development (1976a).

million; the actual cost of the completed half of the project was $419 million (McKay 1984: 62-3).[5]

To some extent, these cost overruns reflect the lack of incentives for cost control in cost-plus contracts. It is not unknown for firms in Ontario to pad their costs, either by doing work of the required quality but overcharging for it, or by doing work of a quality lower than that upon which the contract price was based. For example, at Ontario Hydro's Bruce Heavy Water Plant B 'snow removal costs for two winters totalled $4 million, although equipment was supplied free by Hydro; spending on temporary roads, power and accommodation was projected at over $100 million; a construction company could only account for half of the 1.2 million cubic yards of back-fill it purchased; ... productivity levels dropped below 50 percent and the data were manipulated to conceal the problem' (McKay 1983: 62). The Ministry of Agriculture and Food paid over $34,000 for computer programming under a contract with a public accounting firm. The resulting system was unreliable; it was later replaced by a microcomputer programmed by a summer student. Under the same project, the firm billed for work performed primarily by accountancy student trainees at rates of $35 to $55 per hour; moreover, the number of accountants assigned to the project 'was often disproportionate to the actual work available' (Provincial Auditor of Ontario 1983: 150-2).

Similar in its effect to cost inflation is a contractor's deliberate failure to meet the project's specifications. By producing an output of a quality lower then the quality required under the contract, the firm can lowers its costs and, on a fixed-price project, raise its profits. This problem has been stressed by the provincial auditor: 'In the course of an audit of the Ministry [of Government Services], we examined the extent to which economy and efficiency were observed in the construction of government-owned accommodation. We reviewed a number of projects which had experienced delays, ranging from several months to several years, or had been completed but were deemed unsatisfactory in that they were nonfunctional or dysfunctional' (ibid., 51).

Under a cost-plus contract, the amount paid to the contractor depends on the costs he actually incurs. Since the government cannot perfectly monitor the contractor's costs, it is forced to rely on the contractor's own statement of his costs. To guard against the occasional fraudulent firm, the government audits some such cost claims.

While an unsatisfactory output may be the fault of the firm, it may also be the result of inadequate initial project design by the government agency. According to the provincial auditor, poor design specifications are an important source of excessive costs to the government: 'Designs and specifications which do not fully describe all requirements of projects attract bids in amounts insufficient to fulfil actual requirements of the projects. To complete the

5 These cost overruns, large as they are, are dwarfed by those experienced elsewhere. Nuclear power plants in the United States have been subject to cost overruns totalling in the billions of dollars; for some plants the final cost has been more than twelve times the original estimate (*New York Times*, 26 February 1984).

projects, it is then necessary to issue change orders involving extra costs which are not subject to the competitive bidding process. This places the Ministry in a captive position with the contractors and may result in significantly increased costs of the contracts' (ibid., 52). In other words, inadequate project design exacerbates the incentive problem by making it easy for contractors to inflate their costs.

Inadequate project design can occur in any type of project. It is especially a problem, however, in contracting for consulting services. As we noted in Chapter 7, the *Ontario Manual of Administration* requires that, before a consulting project is tendered, 'the requirements of the assignment are documented and clearly understood' and 'the supplier's output can be measured against defined objectives.' Since the output of a consultancy project is information, it may be difficult to state at the outset sufficiently precise criteria for success or failure of the project.

4. GOVERNMENT MORAL HAZARD

The theory developed earlier presumed that only firms act in bad faith, either by padding their costs or by failing to seek savings in costs. However, there can be moral hazard on the government's side as well. Some businessmen see government work as a source of red tape and time-consuming paperwork, capricious decisions, and delayed payments. These problems are seen by the businessmen as being more prevalent in small municipalities and in the smallest federal or provincial agencies than in large federal or provincial agencies with well-established contracting procedures (*Globe and Mail*, 22 May 1984).

The provisions of some government contracts do seem to be one-sided, giving at least the potential for moral hazard on the side of the government agency. For example, the standard construction contract of the Ministry of Government Services contains the following sentences: 'Delay by the Minister in making payments when they become due and payable shall be deemed not to be a breach of Contract by the Minister. Such delay shall entitle the Contractor to interest on any amount more than thirty (30) days overdue at the rate established by the Treasurer of Ontario. 'Should the amount now voted on by the Legislature be at any time expended previous to the completion of the work now contracted, the Contractor shall not be entitled to any further payment for work done until the necessary funds shall have been voted by the Legislature' (Ontario Ministry of Government Services 1983). The contracts of the Ministry of Transportation and Communications have similar provisions. If, after the project is completed, the ministry is late in making payment, the contract is deemed not to be breached; if the payment is more than seven months late, the ministry pays the contractor interest 'for the period from the day next following the expiration of the said seven month period to the date of payment' (Ontario Ministry of Transport and Communications 1982a).

To the extent that firms perceive the government's moral hazard as a problem, the cost of contracts to the government is raised. For example, if the firms expect payments to be slow, they will raise their bids to cover the interest income lost as a result of late payment.

5. COST-PLUS CONTRACTS AND FIXED-PRICE CONTRACTS

The fixed-price contract is the form of contract most commonly used in Ontario. Is its frequency of use justified by the theoretical analysis of Chapter 3? According to the theory, a fixed-price contract is the optimal contract if and only if both of the following conditions hold: (a) the contractor is risk neutral; (b) either all potential contractors have the same expected costs or there are so many bidders that adding one extra bidder would not noticeably lower the probability that any particular firm will submit the lowest bid. Whether or not a firm is risk neutral depends on its particular circumstances, so condition (a) may or may not be satisfied. If the project is small relative to the firm's capacity, and if the firm is engaged in a diverse range of projects, the firm may behave risk neutrally. However, if the firm is dependent for its survival upon government business, and if its product range is not diversified, it is likely to exhibit risk aversion. In any case, condition (b) is unlikely to be satisfied. According to the theory, the fact that in any actual tender there is almost always a range of bids is evidence that different firms usually do have different expected costs; thus the first part of condition (b) is usually not satisfied. The number of bidders for government contracts is usually less than twenty and commonly between three and twelve. These numbers are too small for the amount of bidding competition to be essentially unchanged if an extra firm bids; hence the second part of condition (b) usually fails to be satisfied. Since conditions (a) and (b) must both be satisfied if a fixed-price contract is to be optimal, it can be concluded that a fixed-price contract is usually not optimal. A fixed-price contract induces too little competition in bidding and requires the firm to bear all of the risk: for these reasons, an incentive contract would on average cost the government less than a fixed-price contract. The Ontario government would often be able to save costs by using an incentive contract where it now uses a fixed-price contract. (Recall the savings estimates reported in Chapter 5.)

The advantage of the fixed-price contract is the strong incentive it gives the contractor to minimize costs. As we have already noted, there are two ways in which this incentive effect can be lost if the contract specifications are not adequate. First, if after a contractor is selected the nature of the work is seen to be different from that specified in the contract, the contractor has the right to renegotiate the contract. Once this situation is reached, the advantages of the bidding competition that preceded the awarding of the contract are lost; the contractor has monopolistic power. Second, if the contract's specifications are vaguely worded, so that there are no precise criteria for the success or failure of the project, it may be impossible to establish that a contractor's work is of inadequate quality. Thus a poorly specified fixed-price contract is essentially a cost-plus contract, as far as its incentives are concerned.

The analysis in Chapter 3 showed that a cost-plus contract cannot be optimal. It is always possible to design an incentive contract that will cost the government less than a cost-plus contract (although this incentive contract may be very close to cost-plus; that is it may have a cost-share parameter, α, with a value very close to 1). It is sometimes suggested that projects involving a large amount of uncertainty should be done on a cost-plus basis. The theory shows that this suggestion is incorrect: the larger is the uncertainty, the other things being equal, the larger is the share of risk that should be borne by the government, and so the closer to the cost-plus end of the spectrum is the ideal incentive contract (in other words, the closer to 1 is the optimal cost-share parameter). However, large uncertainty does not justify using a cost-plus contract. The Ontario government uses cost-plus contracts for professional consulting services; the theory suggests that incentive contracts would cost the government less.

During the energy crisis of the 1970s, there was considerable uncertainty about future fuel costs. In response to this uncertainty, the Ministry of Natural Resources used cost-plus contracts for some multi-year projects with large fuel-cost components. Our theoretical analysis suggests that a more cost-effective response to this particular source of uncertainty would have been to offer contingent contracts. The source of the uncertainty was a specific one, and it is as easy for the government to monitor changes in fuel costs as it is for the contractor. Instead of being simply cost-plus, the contract could have been a fixed-price or incentive contract with payment made contingent on the realized fuel costs (see Chapter 3).

6. HOSPITAL FUNDING

There is one context in which an Ontario government agency has actually used something that approximates an incentive contract as defined in Chapter 3. This is in hospital funding by the Ministry of Health.

As Grant Reuber has noted, important incentives questions arise in the funding of hospitals.

Stronger cost-saving incentives ... need to be introduced at the hospital level. At present over half of personal health care costs are accounted for by hospital costs. Moreover, hospital costs have grown more rapidly than most other health costs. Exactly how such incentives can best be introduced is unclear, given the complexities of the organizational and decision-making responsibilities found in any hospital. Such approaches as global budgeting and incentive rewards, which have been tried in Ontario, have evidently had little impact. The incentives have encouraged hospital boards and administrators to avoid budget overruns, but they have offered little incentive to encourage efficiency. The measures have offered little or no incentive to the physician to change his crucial decisions regarding hospital use and length of stay. (Reuber 1980: 107)

The question of how to measure the quality and quantity of hospital output has been much studied.[6] Less intensively studied, but no less important, is the question of incentives for cost control. In the early 1970s, in an attempt to encourage hospitals to reduce their costs, the Ontario Ministry of Health introduced what it called negative incentive reimbursements and positive incentive reimbursements. The negative incentive reimbursements meant that, except in certain cases, hospitals were responsible for meeting any cost overruns in excess of the approved budget. The positive incentive reimbursements meant that, if a hospital under spent its budget, it could keep 10 per cent of the shortfall (Ontario Economic Council 1977, chap. 4). These incentive schemes closely resemble the incentive contracts analysed in Chapter 3; the positive incentive reimbursement is effectively an incentive contract with a cost-share parameter of 0.9.

This experiment with incentive schemes was not successful. The sharing ratio of 0.9 may have offered too weak an incentive to the hospitals to reduce their costs; more savings might have been achieved had the hospitals been allowed to keep a larger fraction of any costs they saved. Moreover, the way in which the incentive schemes were administered tended to negate their incentive effects. The negative incentive reimbursements were supposed to encourage hospitals to hold costs down by making any operating deficit the responsibility of the hospital. In practice, however, hospitals requested funds to cover their deficits and, depending on the availability of ministry funds, the deficits were partially or wholly funded (Provincial Auditor of Ontario 1983: 58). In other words, the ministry subverted its own negative incentive reimbursement scheme. The ministry's practices also undermined its positive incentive reimbursement scheme. A hospital that successfully held down its costs was given an immediate reward in the form of a fraction of the money it saved. But later it was penalized by having its following year's budget reduced: the next year's budget was based on the current year's actual expenditure rather than on budgeted expenditure.

7. THE GUARANTEED UPSET

The Ministry of Government Services has occasionally used, with favourable results, a device called the guaranteed upset construction contract. This contract resembles a one-sided version of the incentive contract as defined in Chapter 3. Under a guaranteed upset contract, if costs are below the target, the savings are shared by the contractor and the government; cost overruns, however, are the

6   See, for example, Culyer (1978).

responsibility of the contractor alone.

A firm is selected on the basis of competitive bids to act as the construction manager. The selected firm and the project's designers then prepare an estimate of the project's cost. Once the government has accepted this cost estimate, it is called the 'guaranteed contract sum.' The contract manager then tenders the various components of the project to subcontractors. If the contract manager succeeds in having the work done for less than the guaranteed contract sum, the savings are shared by the government and the contract manager. The sharing percentages, previously agreed upon, are usually about 70-80 per cent for the government and 20-30 per cent for the contractor. However, if the actual cost exceeds the guaranteed contract sum, the contract manager is liable for the cost overrun up to within one dollar of his fee. The guaranteed upset contract is therefore like an incentive contract if there is a cost underrun but like a fixed-price contract if there is a cost overrun.

The costs for the government of administering a guaranteed upset contract have been the same as those for a cost-plus contract. The government must ensure that the guaranteed contract sum is reasonable, given the project's specifications; that is, that it has not been padded by the construction manager.

9

Domestic Preferences in Government Procurement

It is common for governments' purchasing policies to favour domestic suppliers. This chapter describes the discriminatory procurement policies used by governments in Canada, the United States, and elsewhere and develops a theoretical framework within which the costs and benefits of procurement preferences can be evaluated.

1. THE INTERNATIONAL CONTEXT

In most countries, the largest purchaser of goods and services is the government. There is, therefore, considerable scope for distortion of international trading patterns by governments' preferential procurement policies. [1]

In 1979, the Tokyo Round of Multilateral Trade Negotiations under the General Agreement on Tariffs and Trade produced an Agreement on Government Procurement. Most of the nations participating in the GATT talks did not sign the agreement, but it was signed by Canada, the United States, Japan, and several Western European countries. The agreement has the aim of increasing international competition in the government-procurement market. It sets out rules for the tendering of government purchases, rules designed to ensure that a government's procurement practices do not protect domestic suppliers and do not discriminate among different foreign suppliers. The agreement applies to large government purchases only; moreover, some items are exempt from its provisions. When the agreement came into effect at the start of 1981, it covered an estimated $35 billion worth of government purchases annually (only a fraction of the worldwide government-procurement market, which is estimated to involve hundred of billions of dollars worth of purchases annually).

---

1   The following facts on government procurement in international trade come from Baldwin (1970), Graham (1983), and International Monetary Fund (1979). For some historical information on government procurement preferences, see Viner (1944).

One of the aims of the GATT agreement is to ensure that there is 'transparency' in governments' procedures for procurement; that is, that the rules governments follow are clearly defined and easy for outsiders to observe.

The most straightforward preference policy is simply to offer a price preference to domestic suppliers. Other policies in use in some countries include requiring that bidders for government contracts be citizens or residents of the country, requiring that goods be locally manufactured, inviting only local firms to submit bids rather than advertising for bids, allowing only a short time limit for the submission of bids, and defining technical specifications in a way that excludes foreign suppliers.

The GATT agreement maintains that governments' procurement practices should follow a principle of non-discrimination: they should allow any foreign supplier to compete on equal terms with either a domestic supplier or a supplier from any other foreign country. Governments may make exceptions to the non-discrimination principle in order to give special advantages to developing countries. The agreement requires its signatories to base the technical specifications of projects on international standards, so that a project's design cannot be used to exclude foreign competitors. It also requires governments not to use the qualification requirements that firms must satisfy before their bids are accepted to exclude foreign firms from bidding. Information on tenders should be made freely available. The contract should be awarded to the lowest bidder capable of doing the work.

Since only federal governments are party to any GATT agreement, the provisions do not bind state governments in the United States or provincial governments in Canada.

The US federal government has long had 'Buy-American' legislation. Its basic provision is a 6 per cent price preference for domestic products; this preference can be raised to 12 per cent in order to favour small businesses or firms in regions of high unemployment.

The Buy-American legislation has special provisions for military items. A special price preference of 50 per cent is granted to US firms contracting with the Department of Defense (DOD). However, most Canadian products are not subject to discrimination under the Buy-American legislation. Similarly, the United States has signed a number of reciprocal agreements with individual countries that exempt the signatories from the Buy-American legislation. The procurement of certain foreign products by the Department of Defense is prohibited. The list includes food, clothing, stainless steel, and buses. The DOD must prefer American contractors for research and development. The Navy's ships must be built in American shipyards using American components. Any contract involving steel must be bid for by at least one American firm. While undoubtedly there is a pork-barrel element to these restrictions, there is at least some partial justification for price preferences on military items. This is the familiar national-defence argument for tariffs, which asserts that a tariff may be justified if it fosters the survival of domestic firms producing essential items whose supply would be cut off in time of war.

Many state governments in the United States have procurement policies that favour local suppliers over out-of-state suppliers. Because of constitutional provisions establishing the freedom of trade across state borders, these state policies have come under frequent attack in the courts. As a result, state legislatures have been forced to enact their procurement preferences into law instead of just applying preferences administratively by, for example, arbitrarily awarding contracts to local suppliers. Many states have statutes that give preference to local suppliers. Some states also have reciprocal preference schemes: the state gives preference to suppliers from certain states in return for its own suppliers' being granted similar preferences by those states.

Governments sometimes use preferential procurement regulations to achieve objectives other than the protection of local industry against foreign competition. The US government has about eighty programs under which it uses the procurement process to further particular socioeconomic objectives. For example, at least 10 per cent of the money spent on federally funded public works projects must go to minority-controlled companies. This regulation was designed to combat racial discrimination in the construction industry. Large construction contractors are required to subcontract a share of their work to companies owned by blacks, Hispanics, Asians, or members of other minority groups. In practice, firms have found these regulations relatively easy to circumvent. Again, the government sometimes shows favouritism to small business. The Small Business Administration sets aside some procurement funds to be awarded to 'socially and economically disadvantaged companies. 'Contracts awarded under this program are not subject to competitive bidding. A third example of the use of procurement to promote specific socioeconomic goals is the direction of procurement funds to regions where unemployment is high (*New York Times*, 1 July 1984; United States 1984, v. 3: 327, v. 8: 95-6). It remains an open question how much it costs the US government to use its procurement policy to further social and political ends.

The Canadian federal government uses its procurement practices to further particular political goals. For example, in undertaking a fifteen-year $3.5 billion project to modernize the country's air-traffic-control network, the government refused bids from foreign companies if enough Canadian companies submitted bids, gave bidders an extra profit margin of as much as 5 per cent in return for increased Canadian content, gave small companies incentives to participate, offered foreign firms the same preferential treatment as Canadian firms in exchange for technology transfers and licensed production within Canada, and gave preference to firms offering research activity and jobs in depressed regions. The weight assigned to each objective was flexible, depending on immediate political priorities. As one report noted, 'the subject of price seemed lost amid the crowd of other criteria' (*Globe and Mail*, 26 April 1984).

2. THE CANADIAN ECONOMIC UNION

The 'Canadian Economic Union' is a term used to describe the idea of a freely operating internal Canadian market, with all barriers to trade in goods and services abolished.[2] Although an attempt was made by the federal government to enshrine the economic-union idea in the Canadian constitution of 1982, the attempt failed in the face of objections from the provincial governments. While tariff barriers between provinces are barred by the constitution, other kinds of barriers to trade, including government procurement preferences, remain legal.

All ten Canadian provinces have guidelines or regulations giving preferences to local suppliers. As we noted in Chapter 7, the Ontario regulations allow a 10 per cent price preference on all 'Canadian content' (that is, all value added in Canada) in the bid. The regulations do not explicitly favour Ontario content over non-Ontario Canadian content; however, the government allows itself to exercise its discretion, and there is one clear instance in which it gave preference to an Ontario supplier: in 1977 and 1983 contracts for streetcar construction were awarded to an Ontario firm even though a Quebec firm was the lowest bidder. (These were cabinet decisions: the *Ontario Manual of Administration* states explicitly that all Canadian firms are to be treated equally.)

Such exceptions aside, the Ontario government's policies are more liberal than those of the other provinces: whereas the Ontario government's regulations specify preferences for Canadian content, the other provinces' regulations protect provincial content. Policies used in other provinces include price preferences of 10 per cent for goods produced within the province: preferences for the use of local labour and local resources; rejection of bids from outside the province if at least three bids are received from within the province; government assistance to create local suppliers if none currently exist; discretionary decision-making power for the government purchasing agent; acceptance of bids from within-province firms even if they are higher than bids of out-of-province firms if this step promotes 'provincial industrial development objectives' (although this phrase is not defined); and requiring that for certain specified items only sources within the province can be used. Such policies can result in a considerable restriction of interprovincial trade. For example, over 90 per cent of the Alberta government's purchases in 1975-76 were from Alberta companies.

3. PROCUREMENT PREFERENCES ARE NOT TARIFFS

Government procurement preferences are sometimes compared to tariffs. Just as there is a tariff rate that is equivalent in its protective effects to any given quota, so, it is suggested, any government procurement preference has its tariff

2   The following facts on the Canadian Economic Union come from Courchene (1984), from Trebilcock, Whalley, Rogerson, and Ness (1983), and from information supplied by the Canadian Construction Association.

equivalent.

For example, Lowinger (1976) used the tariff analogy in attempting to estimate the welfare losses resulting from the US government's procurement policies. Lowinger stated that discriminatory government purchases 'create a wedge between the domestic price and the world market price of internationally traded commodities. By affecting the relative "effective" price of internationally traded goods, the "Buy American" policy causes distortions in the allocation of resources in much the same way that a tariff does.'3 His method was to compute how much the government would import if it had the same propensity to import as the private sector has. Lowinger used this result as an estimate of how much the government would import were there no domestic procurement preferences. He then compared this hypothetical level of government imports with the actual level. Finally, he computed the tariff equivalent to the procurement preferences by computing the tariff rate that would result in a reduction of imports equal to the difference between the hypothetical and the actual government imports (given an estimate of the aggregate price elasticity of demand for imports). Lowinger estimated that the tariff equivalent to US government procurement preferences was a tariff rate between 26 per cent and 43 per cent. This figure was much above existing actual tariff rates (which were mostly below 10 per cent). If this estimate of the impact of government procurement preferences was correct, then the welfare losses suffered by the country's citizens as a result of that impact were very large.

We shall argue in the theoretical analysis developed in this chapter that Lowinger's reasoning is incorrect. It is a mistake to evaluate the effects of government procurement preferences by comparing them to tariffs. The estimates of welfare losses obtained by following this analogy may greatly overestimate the social costs of government preferences.

The conventional economic analysis of the effects of tariffs assumes that a perfectly competitive market prevails: no buyer or seller is a large enough part of the market to have a significant effect on the price that rules in the market. The conventional analysis also depicts all buyers and sellers as being perfectly informed about prevailing prices, so that the 'law of one price' holds: for any particular commodity, ignoring the effects of tariffs and transportation costs, a single price rules everywhere in the world. Given these assumptions, one can show that the ideal tariff rate is zero: a country only lowers its own welfare by imposing tariffs.4 One can then compare actual tariff policies with this zero-tariff ideal in order to compute the welfare losses imposed by tariffs.

While this model of a perfectly competitive, full-information world is adequate for examining some issues in international economics, it is not adequate for examining government procurement preferences. Government purchases do not take place in an environment of many small buyers and many

---

3   Lowinger (1976: 451). Herander (1982) also makes use of the tariff analogy.
4   The argument is summarized in, for example, Harris and Cox (1984: 10-20).

small sellers; instead, there is market power on both sides of the market. The government is the sole buyer. (This is obviously true if the government is procuring, say, a highway. But it may also be true when the government procures standard items such as cars, since the government usually specifies its needs as a package, such as a fleet of cars with particular characteristics.) Because the government is the sole buyer, it has some power to dictate the terms of the purchase. On the other side of the market, there are typically only a few potential sellers—few enough that they can behave strategically towards each other.

Nor is the standard model's assumption of full information adequate: it assumes away an essential aspect of the question of government procurement, namely the government's costs of information gathering. If there were no such costs, the government would not have to call for tenders. Instead, it would simply order the item from the lowest-cost supplier. If the government had full information, it would know who the lowest-cost supplier was, and it could costlessly monitor the chosen supplier's actions so that there would be no question of the firm's inflating its costs. If information costs are significant, one cannot presume that the law of one price holds.[5] In the context of government procurement, the failure of this presumption means simply that bid prices will vary from supplier to supplier.

There is one further way in which government procurement preferences differ from tariffs. A tariff raises the price within the country, so that consumers pay a higher price. While government procurement preferences may (or, as we shall show, may not) raise the price paid by the government, they have no direct effect on the price paid for the item by domestic consumers. Thus one of the important sources of the welfare loss from tariffs, the distortion imposed on consumers' choices, is not present with government procurement preferences.

Since the assumptions of the standard model fail to describe the government-procurement market, the conclusions of the standard model do not apply. Specifically, because the government is the sole buyer, because the suppliers behave strategically, and because uncertainty and information costs are significant, the presumption in favour of free trade disappears. One cannot presume that it is against a country's interests to discriminate against foreign suppliers. As the theory we shall develop will show, in some circumstances government procurement preferences can raise a nation's or a province's level of welfare.

4. QUANTITATIVE EFFECTS OF ONTARIO PREFERENCES

Before we turn to the theoretical analysis of the effects of domestic procurement

5   For models of equilibrium price dispersion owing to buyers' information costs, see Carlson and McAfee (1983), McMillan and Morgan (1983), and the references therein.

preferences, let us consider the size of the effects of the existing Ontario preferences.[6]

Table 9.1 presents data on a sample of contracts awarded by Ontario ministries or other Ontario government agencies on the basis of the province's domestic-preference policy; that is, the lowest bid was rejected in favour of a higher bid with more Canadian content.

Table 9.1 shows how the domestic-preference criterion is applied. For example, the lowest bid of the first contract included $108,022 worth of Canadian content (column 2). Ten per cent of this amount is $10,802. Subtracting the latter amount from the total bid of $124,527 (column 1) gives $113,725: this is the amount reported in column 4 as the 'evaluated bid'; that is, the bid with which the ministry computed the other firms' bids. The amount by which the successful bid exceeded the lowest bid varied from 0.0 per cent to 7.9 per cent of the size of the bid; the average difference was 1.1 per cent of the bid (column 10).

It is important to note that the extent to which the successful bid exceeds the lowest bid does not measure the costs of operating the domestic-preference policy. As we shall argue in detail in the theoretical analysis, the domestic-preference policy affects the way firms bid. Firms with a high Canadian content face weaker competition as a result of the domestic-preference policy and so tend to bid higher. Firms with less Canadian content face stronger competition and as a result are forced to bid lower. The lowest bidder (and, for that matter, every other bidder) would have bid a different amount had the domestic-preference policy not been in force. Indeed, it is possible that the lowest bidder would have bid so much higher in the absence of the domestic-preference policy that the successful bid under the domestic-preference policy is lower than what would have been the lowest bid if there were no preference policy. In short, it is possible that in some instances the domestic-preference policy has the effect of reducing the government's payment. (The theoretical analysis will derive precise conditions under which this would happen; in other cases, the domestic-preference policy might increase the government's payment.) Thus the figures reported in columns 9 and 10 of Table 9.1 should be treated with caution: comparing the lowest bid with the selected bid does not measure the cost to the government of operating its domestic-preference policy.

5. THEORETICAL ANALYSIS OF DOMESTIC PREFERENCES

The following analysis of government contracting in the presence of domestic price preferences is similar to the analysis in Chapter 3. According to that analysis, the optimal cost-share parameter strikes a balance between the degree of incentive it gives to the contractor to hold his costs down and its effect on

---

6   We are grateful to Mr T. Spearin of the Office of Procurement Policy, Ontario Ministry of Industry and Trade, for supplying the information reported in Table 9.1.

TABLE 9.1
Examples of contracts awarded by Ontario ministries and other public bodies in Ontario where Canadian preference policy had an effect on the choice of bidder

Item tendered	Lowest bid			Evaluated bid ($) (4)	Awarded bid			Evaluated bid ($) (8)	Difference	
	Amount of bid ($) (1)	Canadian content $ (2)	% (3)		Amount of bid ($) (5)	Canadian content $ (6)	% (7)		$ (9)	% (10)
Truck dump bodies	124,527	108,022	86	113,725	124,970	115,678	92	113,403	443	0.4
Plastic bindings	3,301	2,409	73	3,060	3,307	2,689	81	3,038	6	0.2
Traffic paint	627,046	572,453	87	572,453	631,071	605,828	96	570,489	4,025	0.6
Signal equipment	46,826	16,908	36	43,135	47,909	47,909	100	43,118	1,083	2.3
Mbl. radio system	385,913	244,875	63	361,428	392,203	325,953	83	359,608	6,290	1.6
Traffic control cables	4,463	2,502	56	4,213	4,621	4,621	100	4,159	158	3.5
Dishwasher	3,695	not provided		3,695	3,920	3,253	83	3,595	225	6.0
EDP cards	139,928	128,734	92	127,055	141,155	141,155	100	127,040	1,226	0.9
Dual brake control	10,366	1,521	14	10,214	10,528	4,428	42	10,085	161	1.6
Office supplies	5,292	not provided		5,292	5,710	5,710	100	5,139	418	7.9
Truck	34,602	8,880	26	33,714	35,040	31,800	91	31,860	438	1.3
Monitors (TV)	3,136	784	25	3,058	3,360	3,360	100	3,024	224	7.1
Typewriters	20,500	8,500	41.5	19,650	20,505	17,181	84	18,787	5	0.0
Fork lift	28,381	12,771	45	27,104	28,508	18,619	65	26,646	127	0.4
Snowmobile	2,501	927	37	2,408	2,590	2,062	80	2,384	89	3.5
Snowmobile	3,120	712	23	3,049	3,144	2,468	79	2,897	24	0.8
Utility uniforms	19,918	9,850	49	18,933	20,540	20,540	100	18,486	622	3.1
Film	496	188	38	477	497	236	47	474	1	0.2
Aerial bucket	91,435	46,824	51	86,753	92,769	89,969	97	83,772	1,344	1.5
Garbage packer	24,036	6,450	27	23,391	24,979	22,721	90	22,707	943	3.9
TOTAL	1,579,482	1,146,791	72	1,462,796	1,597,326	1,466,180	92	1,450,671	17,852	1.1

SOURCE: Data supplied by the Office of Procurement Policy, Ontario Ministry of Industry and Trade.
NOTE: Column 9 is column 5 minus column 1. Column 4 is column 1 minus 10% of column 2. Column 8 is column 5 minus 10% of column 6.

both the contractor's share of the risk and the level of bidding competition among the potential contractors. The only aspect of the earlier analysis that changes when domestic price preferences are introduced is the bidding competition: the bidding-competition effect becomes more difficult to analyse.

Suppose there are two types of firms, domestic and foreign. (For the sake of simplicity, this section's discussion assumes that any bid has either 100 per cent local or 100 per cent foreign content, although, as Table 9.1 shows, this is an oversimplification.) Because the conditions of production—the wage rates a firm must pay, the scale of a typical firm's operations, the state of technology, and so on—differ from country to country, a domestic firm's cost of undertaking a particular project will, on average, be different from a foreign firm's. The mean and the variance of the domestic firms' expected costs will differ from those of the foreign firms. What our analysis will show is that, in principle, the government can, by a calculated use of its price-preference policy, take advantage of these inherent differences between domestic and foreign firms to lower the amount it must pay to have a project completed. Domestic price preferences can be used to increase the amount of bidding competition between domestic and foreign firms.

A price-preference policy pairs off foreign and domestic bids in a particular way. For example, the Ontario 10 per cent price preference means that a domestic firm with a bid of b_1 will beat a foreign firm with a bid of $0.9b_1$ or greater. For the purposes of the theoretical analysis, consider a hypothetical price-preference policy that is somewhat more subtle than the Ontario or any other currently used price-preference policy. Represent the price-preference policy by a function, δ, that induces a comparison between domestic and foreign bids. Specifically, suppose that a domestic bid of b_1 is accepted over a foreign bid of b_2 if $\delta(b_1)$ is less than b_2. Then a preference for domestic firms is indicated if $\delta(b_1)$ is less than b_1 for all possible domestic bids b_1; thus a higher-priced domestic firm could be chosen instead of a lower-priced foreign firm. The current Ontario policy is a particular instance of this hypothetical price-preference policy: in the Ontario case, the function $\delta(b_1)$ is $0.9b_1$ (since domestic bids are reduced by 10 per cent before they are compared with foreign bids).

It is proved in McAfee and McMillan (1985) that a low-cost domestic firm will bid lower than a high-cost domestic firm. Similarly, a low-cost foreign firm will bid lower than a high-cost foreign firm. Thus, as in the model of Chapter 3, bids reveal relative expected costs. But this cost revelation works only in a limited sense. Because domestic firms and foreign firms have different costs on average a low-cost domestic firm will not necessarily bid lower than a high-cost foreign firm (even in the absence of a price-preference policy), or vice versa. The price-preference policy affects the way in which the government compares domestic and foreign firms.

Giving preferential treatment to domestic firms tends to raise the bids of domestic firms (because they now face weaker competition) and lower the bids of foreign firms (because they now face stronger competition). Whether a price-preference policy lowers or raises the government's expected payment depends on whether the latter effect is bigger or smaller than the former effect. The size of each depends in part on how much competition there is within classes: how much competition domestic firms face from other domestic firms, and how much competition foreign firms face from other foreign firms. It is the relative sizes of these two intra-class competition effects that determines whether a price-preference policy favouring local suppliers will lower the government's expected payment.

Suppose that, while some of the domestic firms may be more efficient than some of the foreign firms, the domestic firms have higher production costs on average. What is the effect of a price preference for the domestic firms? The analysis in McAfee and McMillan (1985) shows that if the domestic firms have, on average, higher production costs the effects of the price preference can be to lower the government's procurement costs.

This result follows because, in the absence of the preferential policy, the firms whose average production costs are high impose only weak competitive pressure on the firms whose average production costs are low. A price preference artificially makes the high-cost firms more competitive, forcing the low-cost firms to bid lower than they would otherwise bid. When the price preference leads the government to award the contract to a high-cost domestic firm, its procurement costs are higher than they would be in the absence of the preferential policy. But when the government awards the contract to a low-cost foreign firm, its procurement costs are lower, because the preferential policy has forced the successful firm to bid lower than it would bid in the absence of the policy. With optimally chosen price preferences, the second effect outweighs the first: in net terms the price-preference policy lowers the government's contracting costs.

In McAfee and McMillan (1985) we derived a formula for the optimal size of these price preferences. When the optimal price preference is in effect, the bidding proceeds as if all of the domestic bidders have had their production costs reduced by some fixed amount. The ideal size of the preference will vary from contract to contract.

Not surprisingly, price preferences increase both the number of contracts won by domestic firms and the profitability of those firms. Thus if the domestic industry's production costs are higher than the foreign industry's costs, price preferences, if implemented in a calculated fashion, will simultaneously aid domestic companies and lower the government's contracting costs. It may seem that this conclusion contradicts the economist's often repeated warning against expecting free lunches, but in fact there is no contradiction: if a current policy is suboptimal, it is generally possible to find some change beneficial to some of the participants.

If the highest possible cost for a domestic firm is higher than the highest possible cost for a foreign firm, then the price-preference policy should not involve such strong favouritism that the highest-cost domestic firm will have a chance of winning the contract if it enters a bid. That is, if the domestic firms have higher costs than the foreign firms, it is never optimal for the government to award the contract to the most expensive of the domestic firms. However, if the domestic firms have higher costs on average than do the foreign firms, it is optimal for the price-preference policy to result in a positive probability that the contract will be awarded to a domestic firm with a higher bid than the lowest foreign firm's bid. (Again, the reason for this outcome is that the price-preference policy increases the bidding competition and so can lower some firms' bids.)

Thus the price-preference policy that minimizes the government's expected payment does have a 'protectionist' effect if the domestic firms' costs are higher on average than the foreign firms' costs. The protectionist effect is that the optimal price-preference policy raises the probability that a domestic firm rather than a foreign firm is awarded the contract. The policy also raises the overall profits of the domestic industry. Note the sharp contrast with the tariff, which achieves its protectionist effect by raising prices. If the price-preference policy is optimal, the 'protectionist' effect (the increased probability that a domestic firm wins the contract) is accompanied by a lowering of the expected price for the item.

In some circumstances, the government would minimize its expected payment by operating a price-preference policy in reverse: by favouring foreign firms over domestic firms. This policy is optimal if the foreign firms have higher average costs than the domestic firms; that is, if the local industry has a comparative advantage.

The theory shows that the optimal extent of price preferences varies from project to project. In particular, it depends on how many foreign and domestic firms are likely to enter the bidding, and on the distributions of both the foreign firms' and the domestic firms' expected costs. Moreover, when the domestic producers have a comparative advantage in producing a particular item, the policy that minimizes the government's payments favours the foreign suppliers. Thus a recommendation that emerges from the theory is that any price-preference policy should be applied as flexibly as possible. A rigid policy, such as the Ontario government's 10 per cent price preference, does not take full advantage of the gains to be had from discriminating between domestic firms and foreign firms; indeed, it may often work against the government's interest.

The analysis so far has presumed that the government's objective is simply to minimize its expected payment for the project. Suppose instead that the government has a broader objective: to maximize domestic social welfare. The nationality of the firm that wins the contract has no direct effect on consumers' well-being, so there is no need to include consumption effects in our social-welfare calculations. It may be argued, however, that the government should take account of the expected profits of the domestic firms, because domestic profits affect some citizens' incomes, while foreign profits do not. Suppose, therefore, that the government seeks to maximize expected domestic profits minus its own expected payment. Given this alternative objective, the earlier recommendation is simplified: now the domestic producers should be favoured even if they enjoy a comparative advantage in producing the item.

6. EXCLUSION OF FOREIGN BIDDERS

Price preference is only one of many discriminatory purchasing policies used by governments around the world. As we noted earlier, some countries allow only domestic firms to submit bids. The methods used to exclude foreign bidders include residence requirements, selective-tender or single-tender bidding schemes, short time limits for the submission of bids, and the specification of technical requirements in a way that makes it difficult or impossible for foreign firms to comply.

The theory just sketched applies only to the price-preference policy. However, the theory developed in Chapter 3 can be used to measure the consequences for the size of the government's payment of restrictive tendering policies. The exclusion of foreign firms lowers the number of bidders and so reduces the amount of bidding competition. The simulations reported in Chapter 4 showed that reducing the number of bidders can result in a large increase in the government's expected payment.

7. THE ADVANTAGE OF INCUMBENCY

The advantage of theory is its generality: the same theory can often be applied to different situations. This section applies the preceding analysis in a different context. Possession of a current government contract, or incumbency, often confers a distinct advantage on a firm that is bidding for a new contract of the same type. The government can use its knowledge of the incumbent's advantage to lower its total cost, much as it can lower its total cost when it knows that foreigners have an advantage. The effective means in either case is price discrimination.

While it is generally accepted that an incumbent possesses an advantage in bidding on a new contract, apparently no one has attempted to estimate the magnitude of this advantage or even to prove that it exists. As a result, we must rely on the plausibility of the hypothesis that incumbency is advantageous.

There are several sources of possible advantage to incumbency. First, the incumbent has experience. Consider a project to plant trees in northern Ontario. The incumbent has been engaged by the government to do this in the past, while his rivals have not; he may have learned tricks or strategies that make planting cheaper. For example, the incumbent may be able to make a more informed decision than his rivals can about which equipment will stand up best to the rigours of northern Ontario, or he may have a better idea than his rivals have of the mix of labour and capital that will minimize total costs. In economic parlance, learning by doing can confer an advantage on the incumbent.

A second source of advantage is experience not of the job, but of the process of contracting itself. The incumbent can avoid some bureaucratic pitfalls that the novice cannot. In addition, experienced firms may have more information than their rivals have about the extent to which the government is willing to pay more than the conventional price for particular goods or services. A third advantage of incumbency is that the incumbent may be able to use knowledge of this sort to bring his expected costs below those of less experienced bidders.

In Chapter 3, we observed that a direct government transfer, γ, will lower the bids but leave the same total cost to the government. Suppose a firm knows that if it wins a contract it can charge $1,000 for a 10-cent machine screw. The difference of $999.90 amounts to a transfer to the winning firm. This transfer will not affect the total cost to the government, since bids will drop by $999.90, the amount by which the firms expect to overcharge. There will be an apparent cost overrun of $999.90, but no actual change in expenditure.

This analysis assumes that all of the firms know they can overcharge for the machine screw. If only the incumbent knows, then in general he will lower his bid not by $999.90 but by a smaller amount; his rivals will not lower their bids at all. In this case, because the incumbent knows he can overcharge for the machine screw after he wins, he has, for bidding purposes, a lower cost than his rivals.

In view of these theoretical advantages of incumbency, and in view of the non-systematic, anecdotal evidence that incumbency confers an advantage in bidding for subsequent contracts, we shall presume that such an advantage does exist. As we have seen, when an identifiable class of bidders possesses a cost advantage, it is in the government's interest to reduce this advantage, although not in general to eliminate it completely. While the earlier discussion concerned foreign bidders and domestic bidders, the adjectives can be replaced by 'incumbent' and 'rival' without altering the sense of the argument. In other words, the government can lower its total expected payment by practising price discrimination against incumbents.

Ontario Hydro uses an informal system of price discrimination against incumbents. Ontario Hydro does not seek new bidders unless the incumbent fails to lower his price by a predetermined amount. Thus the incumbent is encouraged by the threat of competitive bidding, to return some or all of the monetary advantages of incumbency to Ontario Hydro in the form of a lower cost for the new project. This two-stage approach is probably preferable to pure price discrimination against the incumbent, since it generally saves the costs of tendering; however, our theoretical model is not able to demonstrate this point with certainty.

A policy of price preference against the incumbent may provide substantial savings in procurement costs for projects, such as road building, that are repeated over a long period of time. It is worth noting that such a strategy lowers costs in precisely the circumstances in which incentive contracting is least useful—that is, when the contractor's risk is very small, as it generally is when he has repeated the same job many times. Consequently, when an incentive contract is not likely to bring the government a significant advantage it should consider using a price preference strategy against the incumbent. (It should be made clear, however, that the two policies are not incompatible.)

There is a second advantage to price discrimination against incumbents, one that does not involve the cost advantages hypothesized at the beginning of this section. Consider the position of a firm that has not been involved in government contracting. Because the incumbent firm's chances of winning have been reduced by price preference (although, of course, it still has a better chance than its rivals), our novice firm's chance of winning is enhanced. Thus price discrimination against incumbents serves to encourage entry into the bidding process—and, as we have seen, increased bidding competition tends to lower costs.

Thus there is a twofold advantage to applying a price preference policy against incumbents. First, the policy reduces procurement costs directly by forcing the incumbent to bid lower. Second, the policy encourages entry into the field, and this enhanced competition also tends to lower costs.

Unfortunately, there are no easy rules at hand for determining the size of the optimal price preference for use against an incumbent contractor. It is likely that Ontario Hydro's experience would be informative; however, the detailed information necessary to study this issue empirically is not currently available. In particular, it would be necessary to compare situations in which the incumbents did not lower their costs sufficiently and lost the contract with situations in which the incumbents did lower their costs sufficiently. The relevant data could probably be produced without too much difficulty, but such an undertaking is beyond the scope of the present study. The area remains an important one for both theoretical and experimental enquiry.[7]

8. SUMMARY

Government procurement preferences, in the form of either price preferences or policies that exclude foreign bidders, are an important feature of both international trade and Canadian interprovincial trade.

Some government procurement preferences take the form of excluding foreign bidders. Such policies reduce the amount of bidding competition and so raise the amount the government pays for a project, possibly by a large amount.

---

7 We provide a theoretical analysis of price preferences in sequential contracts in McAfee and McMillan (1985).

Government price preferences operate very differently from tariffs. They do have a protectionist effect, since by increasing the probability that domestic firms will be awarded government contracts they raise the profits of domestic industry. Unlike tariffs, however, they do not necessarily raise domestic prices. Indeed, if optimally applied, price-preference policies can stimulate the bidding competition between foreign and domestic firms sufficiently to reduce the government's expected payment for a project. The price-preference policy will reduce the government's payment if foreign bidders have a comparative advantage in the particular activity. However, when a local industry has a comparative advantage over the rest of the world, the government's payment would be lowered by instituting a reverse preference policy, favouring foreign suppliers over domestic suppliers. (Special concessions given to firms from less-developed countries might be an example of such a policy.)

The theoretical analysis provides a potential basis for econometric work measuring the size of the effects resulting from preferential government procurement policies.

The use of price discrimination or preference against incumbents provides a means of lowering government cost and stimulating competition in procurement. Ontario Hydro currently uses an ingenious method of price discrimination that often saves the cost of tendering on subsequent contracts. A scarcity of data on this topic prevents a precise formulation of the best policy.

10

Privatization

For centuries philosophers, economists, and political scientists have debated what Edmund Burke termed 'one of the finest problems in legislation, namely, to determine what the State ought to take upon itself to direct by the public wisdom, and what it ought to leave, with as little interference as possible, to individual exertion' (quoted in Keynes 1926: 40). This question has recently been revived in the debate over 'privatization.' Does the modern state take too much upon itself? Which commodities should be supplied by the government and which are more efficiently supplied by the private sector? Would some state-run activities, such as the railways, be better managed if they were sold to the private sector? Even if it has been argued that the public sector rather than the private sector should provide some particular commodity, there is a second and quite separate decision to be made: should the commodity be produced in-house by a government agency, or should its production be contracted out to some private firm? Could some of the activities currently undertaken by government agencies be performed more efficiently by private firms under contract?

1. PUBLIC GOODS AND NATURAL MONOPOLIES

The most important idea in Adam Smith's *Wealth of Nations* is the recognition that the market is the most efficient mechanism for delivering ordinary goods and services into the hands of consumers. The price system mediates between producers and consumers. For example if consumers want more of some item than is being produced, the price will rise and make it worth the producers' while to produce more: the price system itself rectifies the shortage. The price system works by generating appropriate incentives—by creating a coincidence between what is in an individual's self-interest and what advances the social good. Smith put it in this manner:

As every individual, therefore, endeavours as much as he can both to employ his capital in the support of domestic industry, and so to direct that industry that its produce may be of the greatest value; every individual necessarily labours to render the annual revenue of the society as great as he can. He generally, indeed, neither intends to promote the public interest, nor knows how much he is promoting it ... By directing that industry in such a manner as its produce may be of the greatest value, he intends only his own gain, and he is in this, as in many other cases, led by an invisible hand to promote an end which was no part of his intention. By pursuing his own interest he frequently promotes that of society more effectually than when he really intends to promote it. (Smith 1976, Book I: 477-8)

As Smith himself pointed out, however, not all goods and services can be effectively supplied by the market. No one would suggest, for example, that national defence be left for the market to provide. National defence is an example of a *public good*.

A public good has two defining characteristics. The first is *collective consumption*: all individuals in society enjoy the total quantity available of the public good. The public good is not used up when one individual makes use of it. Thus one citizen's benefiting from a system of national defence does not reduce the amount of national defence available for other citizens to benefit from. By contrast, one individual's consuming of an ordinary private good such as a loaf of bread means that the loaf no longer exists for any other individual to consume.

The second defining characteristic of a public good is *non-excludability*. The producer of a private good can prevent anyone he chooses from consuming it. He can use this power to ensure that all who do consume any amount of the private good he produces pay him in return. Ownership of a loaf of bread, for example, is clearly defined. However, people cannot be excluded from enjoying the benefits of a public good. Thus once a system of national defence is in place, all citizens can take advantage of it whether or not they have paid their share of its cost.

Many commodities only partially satisfy the definition of a public good just given. Thus a road meets the conditions of collective consumption and non-excludability except to the extent that it is congested: congestion means that one extra person's using the road does affect another user's capacity to benefit from it. Technical knowledge satisfies the two criteria unless it is patented: the patent allows the owner of the technical knowledge to exclude from using it those who fail to pay for it.

The market cannot be relied on to supply public goods in appropriate amounts. This is because the coincidence between individual self-interest and the social good identified by Adam Smith breaks down with public goods. If each individual could be induced to subscribe towards the provision of a public good an amount of money equal to the value to the individual of the public good, then a decentralized system would succeed in producing the public good. However, because of the collective-consumption and non-excludability features of the public good, each individual has an incentive to pretend that the public good is worth less to him than it really is. Each has an incentive to be a free-rider on the public good supplied by the others. But all individuals would try to do this, and so the public good would be under-supplied.[1]

For example, if a private firm puts on a fireworks display, it cannot exclude anyone in the vicinity from seeing it, and so no one has an incentive to pay the firm for its display. By contrast, a firm that exhibits a movie can exclude those who do not pay.

One important example of a good subject to the free-rider problem is information. Consider a private company that tests cars for safety. If it finds that car A is safer than car B and sells this information, then anyone who buys the information is in a position to sell it or even give it away. Thus the very act of trying to recover the costs of collecting the information (which might involve wrecking cars) produces competitors.

Since the market mechanism fails to operate properly in the case of public goods, the government may have to involve itself in the provision of such goods. As we have already noted, however, it does not follow that public goods must be produced by the government. A public good might be efficiently produced by a private firm under contract to the government. There is a distinction between public production and private production under public financing and control.

A concept related to the concept of a public good is externality. An externality occurs when the costs and the benefits of an activity do not accrue to the same individual. Pollution is an example. If the government does not impose a tax or fine on firms that pollute the environment, a firm will choose to pollute, for most of the costs of this activity are borne by others (those who breathe the pollution). Another example of an externality occurs when a neighbour plays loud music. The neighbour gets the benefits while you bear the costs. No contracting issues arise in these two examples, for in either case the only issue is the choice of a method by which those who benefit also bear the costs.

Other externality issues may involve contracting. One example is education. It is a widely held belief that citizens obtain benefits from having other citizens well educated. Therefore they should be willing to subsidize others' education. This argument is invoked to justify the forced subsidization of education.

The issue of how to supply education consequently arises. This complex, emotional issue has been examined by a number of authors. (See Davies and MacDonald [1984] for an in-depth examination and also for references.) However, an important point is that the choice is not necessarily limited to one between private and public provision of education (or a mixture of the two). The government could also contract out the education of students through competitive bidding.

---

1   For more on the provision of public goods, see McMillan (1979), Manning, Markusen, and McMillan (1985), and the references therein.

Public goods and externalities provide two types of situations in which Adam Smith's invisible hand fails to operate; natural monopoly provides a third. A natural monopoly occurs when economies of scale result in there being room in the market for only one supplier. More precisely, a natural monopoly results when average production costs decline in such a way that minimum average cost occurs at an output larger than total demand. For example, electricity production and the provision of telephone services have marked economies of scale: increasing the amount of electricity produced allows a producer to use more efficient production methods and thus lowers his per-unit costs. Thus one large firm can charge less than smaller firms, and this circumstance will tend to drive the small firms out of the business. As a result, the large firm becomes a monopoly and, in a laissez-faire economy, can charge high prices. Government intervention of some kind may therefore be warranted. Alternative forms of intervention in response to a natural monopoly are public production (for example, the production of electricity by Ontario Hydro) and private production under government regulation (for example, the price regulation imposed on Bell Telephone). If public production is chosen, part or all of the task may be contracted out (as it is by Ontario Hydro).

2. CONTRACTING EXPERIMENTS

In recent years, governments in both Canada and the United States have experimented with having the private sector supply under contract public goods traditionally produced by the government. Activities that have been contracted out include payroll and personnel services, public relations, voter registration, tax collection, mosquito control, snow clearing, park maintenance, pollution control, transit systems, building, mechanical, and electrical inspection, licensing, zoning and subdivision control, street lighting, education, public health services, hospitals, ambulance services, civil defence, weather forecasting, fire services, flood control, irrigation, electricity supply, and garbage collection (Bish 1984; Borcherding 1979; Savas 1982). The bounty hunters of the Old West provided an example of the contracting out of police services, and certain police services are provided by firms under contract in some modern US municipalities. Even the archetypal government activity, clerical work, has been successfully contracted out to firms (Frech 1976).

Several empirical studies have compared the cost of contracted provision of a service with the cost of direct government provision. One study of the provision of fire services by a firm under contract found that the cost was 47 per cent lower than it would have been had the fire services been provided by the local government. Cost savings came from more efficient use of both personnel and equipment, from a greater readiness to adopt innovations, and from economies of scale (the firm also serviced other cities and achieved administrative savings by controlling the different operations from a single office (Bish 1984)).

A study of solid-waste collection in Canadian municipalities found that private contractors supplied the service for an average of 50.9 per cent less than the government. The firms used better equipment and fewer workers than the government agencies, and paid the workers less. Studies of refuse-collection arrangements in US cities have arrived at similar conclusions (Bish 1984).

Electricity has traditionally been produced in the United States, as in Canada, solely by monopolistic public utility companies. In 1978, however, Congress passed a law that requires utilities to purchase electricity generated by other companies at avoided cost; that is, at a price equal to what it costs the utility to generate electricity in its own plants. This law created a market for electricity. As a result, many companies were created to operate small hydroelectric plants: by 1984, thirty-five such plants were operating in New York State alone. These small hydroelectric plants produce electricity more cheaply than the utilities' nuclear plants. The 1978 law has also spurred the development of alternative power-generation technologies, such as wind power. In Canada, power companies are not required to pay avoided cost, and so no private electricity-generating industry has developed (*New York Times*, 11 March 1984; *Globe and Mail*, 1 June 1984).

In 1972 the Canadian federal cabinet issued its 'make-or-buy' directive, which required that all new mission-oriented research-and-development work funded by federal government departments be contracted out to industry. As a result of this directive, an increased amount of research and development has been contracted out. The make-or-buy policy was intended to increase the private sector's awareness of opportunities for commercial exploitation of the results of federally funded research and development. It was believed that government officials often chose inappropriate research and development projects, and that the work would be better directed in the private sector. It was also believed that some of the research done in the public sector was wasted because government researchers had no incentive to seek users of an innovation, but that the market would give firms such an incentive (Supapol and McFetridge 1982).

Since 1960, the United States Air Force has contracted with a firm to provide support functions for an air force base in Oklahoma. The contract specifies performance standards that the contractor must meet, but does not specify how the work should be done. The contractor's main responsibility is to perform maintenance on the aircraft on the base; other responsibilities include fire protection, housing, transportation, food services, recreation services, and civil engineering. It has been estimated that the contract costs the Air Force 22 per cent less than would the conventional method of having the work done by federal government employees. Savings come from lower manpower requirements and more flexible personnel procedures (United States 1984: III-IS6).

3. CONTRACTING VERSUS IN-HOUSE PRODUCTION

Determining whether a particular public good is better produced by a firm under contract or in-house by a government agency is essentially a matter of solving an incentives problem. There are incentives problems associated with in-house production: bureaucracies face the much-discussed, even clichéed, difficulties of motivating their employees to work efficiently. The theory developed in Chapter 3 showed how to design a contract that will give the contractor incentives to do the work properly. When can contracts be expected to be more efficient than bureaucratic production?

Perhaps the most important measure of how successfully a task can be contracted out is how specifically it can be defined—how precisely output can be measured and how clearly criteria for success or failure can be stated in advance. The more precisely the project can be defined, the better are the chances of having it undertaken successfully by a contractor. Building a road can be precisely defined in terms of engineering specifications. A consulting project investigating, say, the causes of teenage crime cannot be given precise advance specifications.

If a project is imprecisely defined, the contractor will be tempted to do poor work, since it will be difficult for the government to establish that the work is in fact of inferior quality. The government's monitoring costs are correspondingly high. Notice that this particular moral-hazard problem, unlike the moral-hazard problem discussed in Chapter 3, applies whether the contract is fixed-priced, incentive, or cost-plus, and that it is strongest when the contract is fixed-price.

While imprecise project specifications may cause contracting not to work well, it cannot be established on a priori grounds that in-house production would be more efficient than contracting. Imprecise specifications make successful in-house production difficult to achieve as well.

For example, one of the most difficult services to define is quality education. However, the problem of definition applies to public education no less than to private education. Indeed, many parents believe that private education is superior to public education, and show their belief by paying a premium to send their children to private schools. Thus, given a proper incentive structure, competition can indeed force a level of quality higher than government production can provide. Private schools compete for parents' dollars and parents make their decision on the basis of a reputation for quality rather than on the basis of price alone. Thus it may still be in the government's interest to contract out production even when quality is difficult to define; however, the government should not choose the firm on the basis of price alone, but also on the basis of reputation for quality. Governments use this strategy in securing professional consulting services, whose quality is generally difficult to define.

There is a drawback to this procedure that raises another issue in connection with the choice between in-house and contracted-out production.

Imagine what might happen if private schools had to bid for government contracts. Consider the fate of a private school that fails to win a government contract. The school incurs heavy expenses in maintaining sufficient capacity to undertake the contract and yet receives no revenue for its efforts. Thus if the cost of being in a position to bid for the right to do a job is high, the number of firms able to maintain sufficient capacity to do the job will be small. Therefore there will be little competition in bidding and bids will be high. This observation leads to the conclusion that contracting out is not desirable when firms require a large amount of expensive capacity to be able to do the job and this capacity will stand idle if a firm does not win.

Indeed, the number of firms there are capable of doing the work is often crucial to the choice between contracting out and in-house production. A main source of the gains from contracting out is the circumstance that competition for the job among different firms drives the price down. If only one firm is capable of doing the work, this advantage of contracting out is lost: the government must buy from a monopolist, probably at a high price. (However, this outcome would not occur often: unless the required services are highly specialized, it is not likely that they will be within the competence of only a single firm.)

A further point to consider in comparing contracting out with in-house production is the fact that the cost of contracting out is explicit, whereas the cost of in-house production is difficult to observe. Thus contracting out provides useful data for rational decision-making. Moreover, contracting out allows the government to take advantage of specialized knowledge or skills in the private sector.

In some cases, partial contracting out may be appropriate. Suppose that a municipality, persuaded of the benefits of contracting out, puts its refuse-collection services up for tender, awards the contract to the lowest bidder, and then sells its trucks and equipment to that firm (as has in fact happened). Some time later, when the service again comes up for tender, the municipality finds that only one firm, the firm that now owns the equipment, is in a position to bid for the contract. The municipality faces a monopolistic supplier on the second contract award and the price it must pay is, accordingly, high—probably higher than the cost of in-house production would have been. If such a situation is likely to emerge, partially contracting out the work may be preferable to either alternative. The municipality could put the service up for tender but retain ownership of its capital equipment and lease it at a pre-stated price to the successful bidder. This arrangement would eliminate the monopoly power of the incumbent firm in future contract awards. Such a solution is commonly adopted in the private sector when firms contract out work to other firms. In the automobile industry, for example, the firms that produce the automobiles retain ownership of the specialized tools, dies, jigs, and patterns used by their subcontractors in manufacturing the components (Monteverde and Teece 1982).[2]

2 See McAfee and McMillan (1985) for a theoretical analysis of sequential contracting with specific assets.

This measure eliminates the possibility that the subcontractor will exert monopoly power after the relationship has been established.

The government's decision whether to have a firm produce a service under contract can be made rationally only on a case-by-case basis, by weighing the cost of government provision against the cost of contract provision.[3]

4. OPTIMAL RESERVE PRICES

Suppose the government has the capability of undertaking a project itself and there are several firms that could also do the work. When should the work be contracted out? The answer is not the obvious one: the government should not contract the work out merely because the private sector can do the work at the same level of quality and with a lower production cost than the government can. Rather, the government's cost-minimizing strategy requires it sometimes to do the work in-house even though its in-house production cost is higher than the production cost of one or more of the bidding firms would have been.

If the government itself has the capability of doing the work, it can use in-house production as a threat to induce the firms to lower their bids. It can do this by using the equivalent of a reserve price in an auction. When the government announces the upcoming tender, it states a reserve price: if it receives no bid lower than the reserve price, it withdraws the tender and does the work itself. Announcing this reserve price may induce the firms to bid lower then they would otherwise bid, thus lowering the cost of the project to the government.

It can be shown that the optimal reserve price is strictly lower than the government's own cost of doing the work. Suppose the government's cost of undertaking some project itself is $100,000. Suppose the lowest possible expected cost a bidding firm could have is $80,000 and the different firms' costs are distributed uniformly. Suppose the contract is put up for tender as a fixed-priced contract. Then it can be shown that the reserve price that minimizes the expected cost to the government (because of its effect on the way the firms bid) is $90,000.

To understand the effect of a reserve price on the firms' bidding, consider two cases. In case 1, the lowest-cost firm that actually enters the bidding has an expected cost of $92,000. In case 2, the lowest-cost bidder has an expected cost of $88,000. In each case, suppose that the firm believes that the second-lowest-cost bidder's cost is more than $5,000 above its own expected cost. Suppose further that in the absence of a reserve price the low-cost firm in case 1 will bid $97,000 and the low-cost firm in case 2 will bid $93,000; that is, each firm will expect to earn a $5,000 profit. Now suppose the reserve price of $90,000 is in

3 For more on the choice between contracting and government production, see Bish (1984), Borcherding (1979), and Savas (1982). For a sceptical opinion of the advantages of contracting out and some anecdotal evidence about poorly designed or poorly administered government contracts, see Hanrahan (1983).

effect. In case 1, no firm can bid below $90,000 without taking a loss: the government receives no bids and must do the work itself at a cost of $100,000, even though, had it not imposed the reserve price, it could have had the work done by the firm for $97,000. This possibility is the disadvantage of imposing the reserve price. In contrast, consider case 2. The lowest-cost firm knows that if it bids above $90,000 it loses the contract and earns no profit. If it bids $89,999, it wins the contract and earns $1,999 profit. Earning $1,999 profit is better than earning no profit. (Recall from Chapter 2 that since the firm's costs include its opportunity costs its potential profits from alternative activities are already taken into account in these calculations.) Thus the firm bids $89,999. Here, then, is the advantage to the government of imposing the reserve price: in case 2, the government pays $89,999 with the reserve price and $93,000 without the reserve price.

One can derive a general formula for this strategy from the economic theory of auctions.[4] As before, let G denote the distribution of firms' expected costs, g the corresponding density function, and α the cost-share parameter. Let c_0 denote the cost of the project if it is done in-house by the government, and let r denote the reserve price, so that all bids are rejected if none are below r. Then the optimal value of r is found by solving the equation

(1) $\quad r = c_0 - (1 - \alpha)G(r)/g(r).$

In particular, suppose that the distribution of the firms' expected costs is uniform — a not unrealistic simplification, as we showed in Chapter 4. Denote the lowest possible expected cost that a firm could have by c_ℓ. Then the formula for the optimal reserve price becomes

(2) $\quad r = [c_0 + (1 - \alpha)c_\ell]/(2 - \alpha).$

It must be the case that $c_\ell < c_0$. Otherwise the government's in-house cost is lower than the lowest possible cost of private production, in which case there is obviously no reason to put the project up for tender. It follows from equation 1 or equation 2 that $r < c_0$. In other words, the reserve price that the government should set in order to minimize its expected cost of having the job done is strictly less than its own in-house production cost. In some instances, then, the government's optimal choice is to do the work itself at a cost higher than the lowest bidder's production cost would have been. Note the simplicity of equations 1 and 2: the optimal reserve price does not depend on the number of firms bidding. In particular, given a fixed-price contract and a uniform distribution of the firms' costs, the optimal reserve price is simply the average of the government's own cost and the lowest-possible expected cost of a firm.

4 Equation 1 can be obtained by combining results from Laffont and Maskin (1980), Riley and Samuelson (1981), and Myerson (1981) (on the optimal reserve price under a fixed-price contract) with results (on the extension to incentive contracts) from McAfee and McMillan (1985).

Why is the optimal reserve price lower than the government's own cost of doing the work? Two opposing effects are at work, as the preceding numerical example showed. The disadvantage of setting the reserve price below the government's own cost is that this policy may result in the government's doing the work when in-house production is more expensive: this result occurs when the lowest bid falls between the reserve price and the government's own cost. The benefit of setting a low reserve price is that it induces firms to bid lower than they would bid otherwise. Clearly a firm will not bid below its own expected costs, but it might be prepared to lower its bid by giving up some of its profits if the alternative is the certainty of not being awarded the contract. The reserve price that minimized the government's expected payment, balancing these two effects, can be shown to satisfy equation 1 or equation 2.

It can also be shown that the government gains nothing by setting a reserve price but keeping it secret (Riley and Samuelson 1981). The optimal strategy for the government is to announce its reserve price openly before the bidding.

The preceding argument demonstrates that comparisons of the costs of public supply and the costs of private supply should be made with care. The fact that the costs of public provision of a particular service are higher than the costs that would have been incurred under private provision is not in itself evidence that the government erred in not contracting the service, because sometimes the government's cost-minimizing strategy requires it to produce in-house even when private production is less costly. Of course, the foregoing argument is relevant only if the project is put up for tender and bids are received before the decision to produce in-house is made.

5. SUMMARY

Public goods are goods that are collectively consumed and from whose benefits no one can be excluded. In the case of private goods, the price system co-ordinates different individuals' wants and needs: self-interest causes people to behave in a way consistent with the social good. In the case of public goods, this coincidence between self-interest and the collective interest breaks down: there is a role for government intervention to ensure that public goods are supplied in appropriate quantities. This intervention may take the form of the government's producing public goods itself, but it need not: instead, public goods may be produced by private firms under contract to the government.

In recent years, many public goods traditionally produced by the government have been successfully contracted out to the private sector, often with substantial cost savings.

Factors that influence the choice between contracted production and in-house production of a public good include the degree of precision with which the project can be defined and the number of firms capable of doing the work. A good or service lends itself to contracting out when many firms are capable of doing the work, the capital outlays necessary are small, and the good or service can be easily defined. Even when quality is difficult to define, selection of a firm on the basis of reputation, rather than on the basis of price alone, may still make contracting out desirable.

If the government is able to do the work itself, then its optimal strategy is to announce a reserve price when it puts a project up for tender. If all of the bids are above the reserve price, the government rejects all of the bids and does the work in-house. The reserve price that minimizes the expected cost of the project to the government is lower than the government's cost of doing the work itself.

11

Summary of Results and Recommendations

It remains to draw together the various strands of the analysis and offer some conclusions.

This study has (1) described and classified the types of contract in use in government-firm contracting; (2) suggested ways in which the most common type of contract, the fixed-price contract, might be used at lower cost to the government, specifically by increasing the amount of competition among firms bidding for the contract; (3) identified the failings of another type of contract sometimes in use, the cost-plus contract, and described an alternative contract that is similar to the cost-plus contract but much less costly for the government; (4) examined the advantages of the incentive contract, which combines features of both the fixed-price contract and the cost-plus contract and, by so doing, ameliorates the disadvantages of both; (5) derived a practical formula for the optimal contract; (6) analysed the consequences of domestic preferences in government procurement; (7) discussed the choice for a government agency between producing a commodity or service in-house and contracting with a private firm for its production; (8) derived optimal reserve-price policies; and (9) examined the experience with contracting of both the Ontario government and the United States Department of Defense, drawing lessons for government contracting in general.

1. THE SIGNIFICANCE OF COST SAVINGS

The simulations in Chapters 4 and 5 suggested that changes in contracting policy could achieve savings for the government of as much as 30 per cent. The size of the savings varies with the particular contracting situation, but 8 per cent is a typical saving.

Are savings on the order of 8 per cent large enough to justify changes in policy? We would argue emphatically that they are. The Ontario government annually spends $9 billion in procuring goods and services from private firms

(Ontario Ministry of Industry and Trade 1984). An 8 per cent reduction in this figure would amount to savings of $720 million, a considerable sum by any reckoning. Moreover, this saving would be achieved repeatedly, year after year.

It is worth comparing these potential savings of around 8 per cent with the provincial budget deficit, about which there is so much popular concern. In 1983 the Ontario budget deficit amounted to 9.8 per cent of total provincial expenditure (Conklin and Courchene 1984: 81). The savings from improved contracting procedures would be much too small to eliminate the budget deficit, but they could reduce it significantly.

2. WAYS OF ACHIEVING SAVINGS

The present study has suggested a number of ways in which the cost to the government of contracted work could be reduced. Some of these cost-saving techniques are already used, wholly or in part, by government agencies; others are original to this study. This section reviews the specific areas in which the government might find opportunities for significant savings.

Definition of project specifications. Poor design specifications are an important source of excessive costs to the government. If the criteria by which the completed project is to be judged are vague, the contractor can, without penalty, do low-quality work. If the project's specifications are revealed during the course of the work to be infeasible, the price for the modified project must be renegotiated—but now, the contractor is in a monopoly position, which he can exploit in the negotiations to obtain a high price. (See Sections 6.3, 6.4, and 8.3.)

The tendering procedure. The use of the sealed-bid tender encourages low bids. Short of a complicated system in which high bidders are penalized and low but unsuccessful bidders are subsidized, the sealed-bid tender is the optimal tendering procedure, yielding lower bids than alternative procedures. This study therefore endorses the almost universal use of the sealed-bid tender by government agencies. (See Sections 2.6 and 7.1.)

Collusion in bidding. There is a temptation for the bidders to combine secretly in an effort to raise prices. Successful collusion can double the price of a project. No contracting procedure can be designed that is immune to collusion; the only answer is for the government agency to be aware of the possibility of collusion and to watch continually for signs of its presence. Encouraging entry of new firms into the industry is one way of reducing the likelihood that collusion will develop or persist. (See Sections 2.7 and 8.2.)

Bidding competition. Bidding competition matters for two reasons. First, the more firms there are bidding for the job, the more each firm's bid will be driven down. Second, unless the contract is a cost-plus contract, bids reveal relative expected costs; that is, the lowest-cost firm bids lowest.

The data presented in this study show that increasing the amount of bidding competition can have a surprisingly large effect on the price paid by the government. In one set of data, the price paid by the government for a given item when there was competition was on average half the price paid for the same item when there was no competition. Simulations of the effect of increasing the number of bidders show a significant cost-saving potential. For example, increasing the number of bidders from 3 to 4 can result in savings of up to 18 per cent; from 7 to 8, up to 4 per cent; and from 10 to 11, up to 2 per cent. Efforts by the government to increase the number of firms bidding for government business can therefore yield a significant payoff.

The government can increase the number of bidders for a project by dividing it into separate projects (presuming such a division is technically feasible). Then small firms can bid for the job—firms that might otherwise be excluded from competing by their capacity constraints. The government can also ensure that there are as many bidders as possible by advertising upcoming contract awards widely, so that all relevant firms know of the opportunity; by allowing a period for the submission of bids long enough to ensure that no firms are excluded for want of time in which to prepare their bids; and by defining the project's technical specifications in as broad terms as possible to that capable firms are not excluded by a failure to satisfy criteria that are not strictly relevant to the project's requirements.

Bidding competition depends not only on the number of bidders; of equal importance is the variance in the firms' expected costs. The closer are the different firms' expected costs, the fiercer is the bidding competition and therefore the lower is the price paid by the government. Thus it is in the government's interest for it to attempt to reduce the inherent cost differences among the firms. For example, the government might publicize new technologies, to ensure that all firms, and not just one or two, are using up-to-date production methods. (See Chapter 4.)

Macroeconomic implications. Firms will bid the lower for any contract the lower are their opportunity costs—that is, the less profitable are their alternatives to that particular contract. Thus the government can lower its total payments by commissioning more work during recessions than it commissions when the economy is booming. As a bonus, such a policy has beneficial macroeconomic effects: to the extent that fiscal policy is effective, an increase in government expenditure tends, in Keynesian fashion, to counteract the ill-effects of a slump. (See Sections 2.1 and 3.13.)

Government as risk bearer. Because the risks of failure of any one government project are spread across all citizens, the cost to society of having the government bear risk is insignificant. Therefore the government should be risk-neutral in the face of uncertainty. If a firm with which the government deals is risk averse, then it will be willing to accept a lower rate of profit in exchange for the government's taking some risk away from it. Thus the government can lower its expected payment by bearing some of the project's risk. Contractual arrangements that relieve the firm of some of the risk are therefore advantageous to the government. (See Section 2.3.)

Ex-post evaluations. The political process tends to evaluate decisions by results. Thus if a project turns out to be unduly costly, the decision that initiated the project is condemned. This tendency to evaluate decisions with the benefit of hindsight is not only unfair but, what is more important, may lead to poor decisions. It may cause government officials to be risk-averse when social efficiency requires them to be risk-neutral. (See Section 2.3.)

Fixed-price contracts. The fixed-price contract is the most commonly used form of government contract in Ontario and in most other jurisdictions as well. According to our theoretical analysis, the fixed-price contract is optimal if and only if (a) the bidders are all risk neutral and (b) either there are very many bidders or all bidders have the same expected costs. If these conditions are not met, an incentive contract would perform better, from the point of view of the government, than would a fixed-price contract. (For more details, see Sections 3.3, 3.4, 3.5, 6.4, 7.3, and 8.5).

Incentive contracts. The incentive contract has the disadvantage, relative to the fixed-price contract, that it gives the contractor weaker incentives to hold down the costs he incurs. In many cases, however, this disadvantage is outweighed by two other considerations. Relative to the fixed-price contract, the incentive contract induces stronger bidding competition among the firms seeking the contract; it also requires the selected firm to bear less risk, so that the firm, if it is risk averse, is willing to accept a lower rate of profit. Both of these effects tend to make the incentive contract less costly for the government than the fixed-price contract. Unless the necessary and sufficient conditions for the optimality of the fixed-price contract are satisfied, the government pays a lower price on average under an incentive contract than it pays under a fixed-price contract. It follows that, in many instances in which fixed-price contracts are now used, using an incentive contract instead would result in savings for the government. We presented a reasonably simple method of computing the optimal cost-share parameter for the incentive contract in Chapter 5. We recommend, therefore, a change in the government's policy: an incentive contract should be used in many (but not all) cases where currently a fixed-price contract is used. Simulations show that savings of as much as 45 per cent, and typically around 8 per cent, can be achieved by using an optimal incentive contract in place of a fixed-price contract. For 60 per cent of the actual Ontario government contracts examined, significant savings could have been achieved had an incentive contract been used instead of a fixed-price contract.

The simplicity of using an incentive contract should be stressed. For the government official, the computation of an approximately optimal cost-share parameter can be reduced to a routine matter. For the firm, working under an incentive contract need be no more difficult than operating under other payment schemes, such as commission or royalty schemes, that make payment contingent on performance. (See Sections 3.3, 3.4, 3.6, Chapter 5, and Sections 6.5, 6.6, 8.6, and 8.7.)

Cost-plus contracts. Cost-plus contracts are unduly costly to the government, for two reasons. First, a cost-plus contract gives the contractor little incentive to keep realized costs low, because any increase in costs is simply passed on to the government. Second, and more subtly, offering a cost-plus contract usually results in the wrong firm's being selected. The bids for a cost-plus contract are not related to true expected costs: a high-cost firm can bid low because it knows that its actual costs, whatever they are, will be covered by the government. Thus a cost-plus contract (unlike a fixed-price contract or an incentive contract) gives the government no reason to presume that by picking the lowest bidder it has picked the lowest-cost firm.

It is always possible to devise an incentive contract that performs better than a cost-plus contract. Even an incentive contract that is very close to a cost-plus contract (for example, an incentive contract with a cost-share parameter set at 95 per cent) will cost the government less than will a cost-plus contract. Such an incentive contract is subject to the first disadvantage of the cost-plus contract: it gives the contractor little incentive to exert effort to keep his costs low. However, it is not subject to the second failing of the cost-plus contract: under any incentive contract, expected costs are relevant to the firm's decision on how low to bid; therefore, the lowest-cost firm bids lowest, so that when the government selects the lowest bidder it does in fact choose the right firm for the job. (See Sections 3.3, 3.4, 3.5, 6.4, 7.3, and 8.5.)

Contingent contracts. If the cost of a project will be affected in an important way by some future event, and if both parties to the contract can observe the event, there are advantages to using a contingent contract—that is, a contract under which the amount of the payment is contingent on the outcome of the unpredictable event. For example, costs may be affected by inflation in input prices; the contract price may therefore be indexed to negate the effects of inflation. The contingent contract is beneficial to both parties. The firm's uncertainty about its profit is reduced; consequently, if the firm is risk averse, it will be willing to accept a lower rate of profit. The cost of the project to the government is therefore lowered.(See Section 3.12.)

The irrelevance of cost overruns. If the contract is optimally designed, cost overruns should not be viewed with concern. The important number is the total cost of the project to the government, not the amount by which final costs exceed target cost. Provided the cost-share parameter is set at its optimal level, what the government loses through cost overruns exactly matches what it gains through lower initial bids. However, with a cost-plus contract (which we have argued, cannot be an optimal contract), firms submit bids that are unrelated to their expected costs: thus cost overruns under cost-plus contracts are symptoms of the inadequacy of such contracts. (See Sections 3.7, 3.8, and 3.9.)

Random auditing. With a cost-plus contract or an incentive contract, but not with a fixed-price contract, the amount ultimately paid to the contractor depends on the costs incurred. The government must therefore have some procedure for auditing contractors' cost statements to guard against fraud. The Ontario government's current policy on cost-plus contracts is to audit completely every cost statement. This is excessive. A more cost-effective strategy is random auditing. The fact that there was some probability of detection would be enough to deter most fraud (just as random auditing of income-tax returns is enough to deter most people from trying to defraud the tax authorities). There is less need to audit incentive contracts than cost-plus contracts, because under an incentive contract the contractor bears some responsibility for his own costs. Thus incentive contracts, while somewhat more costly for the government to administer than fixed-price contracts, are less costly to administer than cost-plus contracts. (See Sections 3.11 and 6.5.)

Sales taxes. The theoretical analysis showed that in net terms the imposition of a sales tax on the inputs used by a contractor costs the government money: the sales tax raises the cost of the project by more than the value of the sales tax collected. This result suggests a policy recommendation: sales taxes on items used in government projects should be rebated. This proposal is a tentative one, however: a rebate policy might generate considerable administrative costs for the government. However, regardless of the question of administrative costs, the point remains that the government lowers rather than raises its net revenue by imposing taxes on contractors' inputs. (See Section 4.5.)

Domestic preferences. The Ontario government offers a 10 per cent price preference for the Canadian content in the good or service being tendered. The US government has a 6 per cent price preference for domestic content. The theoretical analysis showed such a policy may be justified quite apart from any protection it may provide to domestic firms. In some circumstances, a preferential policy might actually lower the price paid by the government by stimulating bidding competition. A policy of favouring bidders with a high domestic content over bidders with a high foreign content is justified purely on the grounds of savings to the government if the foreign producers have a comparative advantage (that is, if the foreign producers have lower costs on .

average than do the domestic producers). This argument must be treated with a great deal of caution, however, for a preferential policy will succeed in stimulating bidding competition only if it is applied in a very flexible and sophisticated way. A simple, unvarying rule (such as Ontario's policy of favouring domestic firms by 10 per cent) may often result in the government's payment being higher rather than lower. Indeed, in an industry in which the domestic producers have a comparative advantage over the foreign producers, the government will minimize its payment by favouring foreign content. (See Chapter 9.)

In-house production versus contracting out. The question of whether a publicly financed commodity is more efficiently produced by the government itself or by a firm under contract is complicated and few general rules can be stated. Ultimately, the question is an empirical one: which mode of supply works best in practice? For this reason, we support the idea of experimenting with the alternative modes of supply, as has been done in recent years in both Canada and the United States. The results of these experiments suggest that it may be to a government's advantage to contract out many of the goods and services that governments have traditionally produced directly. (See Sections 10.1, 10.2, and 10.3.)

Reserve prices. If a government has the capability of undertaking a project itself, its cost-minimizing strategy is to announce a reserve price strictly lower than its own cost of doing the work in-house, with the understanding that if no one submits a bid lower than the reserve price the government will do the work itself. The optimal reserve price can be computed from data on the government's own cost and the distribution of firms' costs. In particular, given a fixed-price contract and a uniform distribution of firm's costs, the optimal reserve price is simply the average of the government's own cost of doing the work and the lowest expected cost that a firm could possibly have. Thus comparisons between the cost of public supply and the cost of private supply should be made with care. The fact that public provision of a particular service is more expensive than private provision would have been is not in itself evidence that the government erred in failing to contract out that service, because the government's cost-minimizing strategy sometimes requires it to produce in-house even when a firm would have lower production costs. (See Section 10.4.)

Comparison with private-sector contracting. The private sector, which is not constrained by the public sector's requirements of visibility and accountability, typically awards contracts by closed negotiations rather than by formal bidding. The advantage of negotiation is that it gives the purchasing agent the flexibility to bargain down prices. One general advantage of the policies advocated by the present study (the use of incentive contracts, price preferences, and reserve prices) is that they would introduce into the operation of the sealed-bid public tender some of the flexibility inherent in closed negotiations. (See Section 1.2.)

References

Aljian, George W., ed. 1958. *Purchasing Handbook*. New York: McGraw-Hill
Appelbaum, E., and A. Ullah. 1983. 'An empirical test of the risk aversion
   hypothesis.' Mimeo. University of Western Ontario
Arrow, Kenneth J., and Robert C. Lind. 1970. 'Uncertainty and the evaluation of
   public investment decisions.' *American Economic Review* 60: 364-78
Bailey, Andrew, James Gerlach, R. Preston McAfee, and Andrew Whinston
   1981a. 'Formal analysis of internal control—an introduction.' *The
   Proceedings of the First European Workshop on Information Systems* (Aix-
   en-Provence)
- 1981b. 'Internal accounting controls in the office of the future.' *Institute of
   Electrical and Electronics Engineers Computer Journal* 14 (no. 5): 59-70
- 1981c. 'An application of complexity theory to the analysis of internal
   control.' *Auditing: A Journal of Practice and Theory* 1 (no. 1): 38-52
- 1982a. 'Office automation.' *Handbook of Industrial Engineering*, ed. Gavriel
   Salvendy. New York: John Wiley & Sons
- 1982b. 'Ticom II—the internal control language.' In Abdel-Khalik, ed.,
   Florida Symposium of Internal Control. Gainesville: University of Florida
   Press
- 1982c. 'An OIS model for internal control evaluation.' *ACM Transactions on
   Office Information Systems*, ACMSIGOA, November, 1 (no. 1): 25-44
Baldwin, Robert E. 1970. *Nontariff Distortions of International Trade*.
   Washington: Brookings Institution
Ballard, Charles L., John B. Shoven, and John Whalley. 1985. 'General
   equilibrium computations of the marginal welfare costs of taxes in the United
   States.' *American Economic Review* 75: 128-38
Baron, David. 1972. 'Incentive contracts and competitive bidding.' *American
   Economic Review* 62: 384-94
Berhold, Marvin. 1971. 'A theory of linear profit-sharing incentives.' *Quarterly
   Journal of Economics* 85: 460-82
Bish, Robert L. 1984. 'Productivity increasing arrangements for producing

government services: the role of contracting out.' Research study prepared for the Royal Commission on the Economic Union and Development Prospects for Canada

Boger, Dan C., Carl R. Jones, and Kevin C. Sontheimer. 1983. 'What are the incentives in incentive contracts?' *Defense Management Journal* 19: 17-22

Borcherding, Thomas E. 1979. 'Towards a positive theory of public sector supply arrangements.' Discussion Paper 79-15-3. Simon Fraser University

Campbell, Harry. 1975. 'Deadweight loss and commodity taxation in Canada. '*Canadian Journal of Economics* 8: 441-6

Carlson, John A., and R. Preston McAfee. 1983. 'Discrete equilibrium price dispersion.' *Journal of Political Economy* 91: 480-93

Cassady, R., Jr. 1967. *Auctions and Auctioneering*. Berkeley: University of California Press

Comanor, W.S., and M.A. Schankerman. 1976. 'Identical bids and cartel behavior.' *Bell Journal of Economics* 7: 281-6

Conklin, David W., and Thomas J. Courchene, eds. 1983. *Deficits: How Big and How Bad?* Toronto: Ontario Economic Council

Courchene, Thomas J. 1984. 'The Canadian economic union.' Research study prepared for the Royal Commission on the Economic Union and Development Prospects for Canada

Crommelin, Michael, Peter H. Pearse, and Anthony Scott. 1978. 'Management of oil and gas resources in Alberta: an economic evaluation of public policy.' *Natural Resources Journal* 18: 337-59

Cross, John G. 1968. 'A reappraisal of cost incentives in defense contracts'. *Western Economic Journal* 6: 205-25

Culyer, A.J. 1978. *Measuring Health: Lessons for Ontario*. Toronto: Ontario Economic Council

Cummins, J.M. 1977. 'Incentive contracting for national defense: a problem of optimal risk sharing.' *Bell Journal of Economics* 8: 168-85

Danhof, Clarence H. 1968. *Government Contracting and Technological Change*. Washington, DC: Brookings Institution

Davies, James, and Glenn MacDonald. 1984. *Information in the Labour Market: Job-Worker Matching and Its Implications for Education in Ontario*. Toronto: Ontario Economic Council

Debreu, Gerard. 1959. *Theory of Value: An Axiomatic Analysis of Economic Equilibrium*. New Haven: Yale University Press

DeMayo, Peter. 1983. 'Bidding on new ship construction.' In R. Engelbrecht-Wiggans, M. Shubik, and R.M. Stark, eds., *Auctions, Bidding and Contracting: Uses and Theory*. New York: New York University Press

Denham, Ross A. 1978. 'New public-sector audit legislation in Canada. *Canadian Public Policy* 4: 474-88

Drèze, Jacques H. 1979. 'Human capital and risk-bearing.' *The Geneva Papers on Risk and Insurance* 12: 5-22

England, Wilbur B. 1970. *Modern Procurement Management*. Homewood,

Ill.: Richard D. Irwin

Feldstein, Paul J. 1983. *Health Care Economics*, 2nd ed. New York: John Wiley & Sons

Fishe, Raymond P.H., and R. Preston McAfee. 1982. 'Contract design under uncertainty.' Mimeo. University of Western Ontario

Fisher, I.N. 1969. 'An evaluation of incentive contracting experience.' *Naval Research Logistics Quarterly* 16: 63-83

Fisher, I.N., and G.R. Hall. 1969. 'Risk and corporate rates of return.' *Quarterly Journal of Economics* 83: 79-92

Fox, J. Ronald. 1974. *Arming America: How the U.S. Buys Weapons*. Cambridge: Harvard University Press.

- 1984. 'Revamping the business of national defense.' *Harvard Business Review* 62: 63-70

Frech, H.E. 1976. 'The property rights theory of the firm: empirical results from a natural experiment.' *Journal of Political Economy* 84: 143-52

Gansler, Jacques S. 1980. *The Defense Industry*. Cambridge: MIT Press

Gaver, Kenneth M., and Jerold L. Zimmermann. 1977. 'An analysis of competitive bidding on BART contracts.' *Journal of Business* 50: 279-95

Gilley, Otis V., and Gordon V. Karels. 1981. 'The competitive effect in bonus bidding: new evidence.' *Bell Journal of Economics* 12: 637-48

Gjesdal, Froystein. 1982. 'Information and incentives: the agency information problem.' *Review of Economic Studies* 49: 373-90

Graham, W.C. 1983. 'Government procurement policies: GATT, the EEC, and the United States.' In M.J. Trebilcock et al., *Federalism and the Canadian Economic Union*. Toronto: Ontario Economic Council

Green, Christopher. 1980. *Canadian Industrial Organization and Policy*. Toronto: McGraw-Hill Ryerson

Grossman, Sanford J., and Oliver D. Hart. 1983. 'An analysis of the principal-agent problem.' *Econometrica* 5: 7-46

Hanrahan, John D. 1983. *Government by Contract*. New York: Norton

Harris, Milton, and Artur Raviv. 1979. 'Optimal incentive contracts with imperfect information.' *Journal of Economic Theory* 20: 231-59

- 1981. 'Allocation mechanisms and the design of auctions.' *Econometrica* 49: 1477-500

Harris, Milton, and Robert M. Townsend. 1985. 'Allocation mechanisms, asymmetric information, and the "revelation principle." In G. Fiewel, ed., *Issues in Contemporary Microeconomics and Welfare*. Albany: State University of New York Press

Harris, Richard G., with David Cox. 1984. *Trade, Industrial Policy, and Canadian Manufacturing*. Toronto: Ontario Economic Council

Haywood, Ralph. 1984. 'Optimal high valuer auctions.' Mimeo. University of California, San Diego

Herander, Mark. 1982. 'The impact of government price discrimination and its equivalence with the tariff.' *Weltwirtschaftliches Archiv* 118: 524-45

Hiller, John R., and Robert D. Tollison. 1978. 'Incentive versus cost-plus contracts in defense procurement.' *Journal of Industrial Economics* 26: 239-48

Holmström, Bengt. 1979. 'Moral hazard and observability.' *Bell Journal of Economics* 10: 74-91

Holt, Charles A., Jr. 1979. 'Uncertainty and the bidding for incentive contracts.' *American Economic Review* 69: 697-705

- 1980. 'Competitive bidding for contracts under alternative auction procedures.' *Journal of Political Economy* 88: 433-45

- 1982. 'Bidding for contracts.' In *Bayesian Analysis in Economic Theory and Time Series Analysis*. Amsterdam: North-Holland

Hurwicz, L. 1972. 'On informationally decentralized systems.' In C.B. McGuire and R. Radner, eds., *Decision and Organization*. Amsterdam: North-Holland

International Monetary Fund. 1979. *IMF Survey*, 7 May

Kamien, Morton I., and Nancy L. Schwartz. 1981. *Dynamic Optimization*. Amsterdam: North-Holland

Keynes, J.M. 1926. *The End of Laissez-Faire*. London: The Hogarth Press

Koch, James V. 1980. *Industrial Organization and Prices*, 2nd ed. Englewood Cliffs, NJ : Prentice-Hall

Laffont, Jean-Jacques, and Eric Maskin. 1980. 'Optimal reservation price in the Vickrey auction.' *Economics Letters* 6: 309-13

Laffont, Jean-Jacques, and Jean Tirole. 1985. 'Using cost observation to regulate firms.' Mimeo. Université de Toulouse

Lee, Tom K. 1984. 'Why do we generally observe quality underruns and cost overruns?' Discussion Paper No. 84-13, University of California, San Diego

Lewis, Tracy R. 1984. 'Reputation and contractual performance in long-term projects.' Discussion Paper No. 84-23, University of British Columbia

Lippman, Steven A., and John J. McCall. 1981. 'The economics of uncertainty: selected topics and probability methods.' In K.J. Arrow and M.D. Intriligator, eds., *Handbook of Mathematical Economics*, Vol. 1. Amsterdam: North-Holland

Lowinger, Thomas C. 1976. 'Discrimination in government procurement of foreign goods in the U.S. and Western Europe.' *Southern Economic Journal* 42: 451-60

Macaulay, Stewart. 1963. 'Non-contractual relations in business: a preliminary study.' *American Sociological Review* 28: 55-67

MacDonald, Glenn. 1984. 'New directions in the economic theory of agency.' *Canadian Journal of Economics* 17: 415-40

Manning, Richard, James R. Markusen, and John McMillan. 1985. 'Paying for public inputs.' *American Economic Review* 75: 235-8

Maskin, Eric, and John Riley. 1980. 'Auctioning an indivisible object.' Mimeo. Massachusetts Institute of Technology

- 1981. 'Monopoly with incomplete information.' Working Paper No. 268,

University of California, Los Angeles
- 1984. 'Optimal auctions with risk averse buyers.' *Econometrica* 52: 1473-1518

Matthews, Steven A. 1983. 'Selling to risk averse buyers with unobservable tastes.' *Journal of Economic Theory* 30: 370-400
- 1984. 'On the implementability of reduced form auctions.' *Econometrica* 52: 1519-23

McAfee, R. Preston. 1983. 'American economic growth and the voyage of Columbus.' *American Economic Review* 73: 735-41
- 1984. 'The nature of risk aversion.' Research Report, University of Western Ontario

McAfee, R. Preston, and John McMillan. 1985. 'Discrimination in Auctions. 'Discussion Paper No. 85-7, University of California, San Diego
- 1986. 'Bidding for contracts: a principal-agent analysis.' *Rand Journal of Economics*, 17: 326-38
- 1987a. 'Auctions with a stochastic number of bidders.' *Journal of Economic Theory*, to appear
- 1987b. 'Search mechanisms.' *Journal of Economic Theory*, to appear.

McCall, John J. 1970. 'The simple economics of incentive contracting.' *American Economic Review* 60: 837-46

McKay, Paul. 1983. *Electric Empire: The Inside Story of Ontario Hydro.* Toronto: Ontario Public Interest Research Group

McMillan, John. 1979. 'The free-rider problem: a survey.' *Economic Record* 55: 95-107
- 1984. 'Collusion, competition, and conjectures.' *Canadian Journal of Economics* 17: 788-805
- 1986. *Game Theory in International Economics.* Paris: Harwood

McMillan, John, and Peter Morgan. 1983. 'Price dispersion, price flexibility, and consumer search.' Research Report, University of Western Ontario

Mead, Walter J. 1967. 'Natural resource disposal policy: oral auction versus sealed bids.' *Natural Resources Journal* 7: 195-224

Milgrom, Paul R., and Robert J. Weber. 1982. 'A theory of auctions and competitive bidding.' *Econometrica* 50: 1089-122

Monteverde, Kirk, and David J. Teece. 1982. 'Appropriate rents and quasi-vertical integration.' *Journal of Law and Economics* 25: 321-9

Moore, F.T. 1967. 'Incentive contracts.' In S. Enke, ed., *Defense Management.* Englewood Cliffs, NJ: Prentice-Hall

Moore, John. 1984. 'Global incentive constraints in auction design. '*Econometrica* 52: 1523-36

Mund, Vernon A. 1969. 'Identical bid prices.' *Journal of Political Economy* 68: 150-69

Myerson, Roger B. 1981. 'Optimal auction design.' *Mathematics of Operations Research* 6: 58-73

Ontario. 1976-83. *Ontario Manual of Administration.* Toronto

162 References

- 1983. *Report of the Standing Committee on Public Accounts*. Toronto
Ontario Economic Council. 1977. *The Process of Public Decision-Making*.
  Toronto
Ontario Hydro. 1977. 'The process of negotiation.' Mimeo. Toronto
- 1981-84. *Purchasing Policies and Procedures Manual*. Toronto
- 1983. *Annual Report of Procurement Activity*. Toronto
Ontario Management Board of Cabinet. 1983. 'Guidelines on the acquisition of
  creative communications services.' Toronto
Ontario Ministry of Government Services. 1983. 'Standard form of construction
  contract for a stipulated sum.' Toronto
Ontario Ministry of Industry and Trade. 1983. *Ontario's $9 Billion Public
  Sector Market: Purchasing Directory and Guide 1983/84*. Toronto
Ontario Ministry of Transportation and Communications. 1977. *Instructions to
  Bidders*. Toronto
- 1982a. *General Conditions for Contractors*. Toronto
- 1982b. *Qualification Procedures for Contractors*. Toronto
- 1983. 'Tender for Contract No. 83-54.' Toronto
- 1984. *Contract Bulletin* (various issues)
Ontario Ministry of Treasury and Economics. 1983a. *Public Accounts 1982-83:
  Financial Statements*. Toronto
- 1983b. *Public Accounts 1982-83: Financial Statements of Crown
  Corporations, Boards, Commissions*. Toronto
- 1983c. *Public Accounts 1982-83: Details of Expenditures*. Toronto
Organization for Economic Co-operation and Development. 1976a. *Collusive
  Tendering*. Paris
- 1976b. *Government Purchasing*. Paris
Osband, Kent, and Stefan Reichelstein. 1984. 'Information eliciting
  compensation schemes.' Working Paper No. EAP-4, University of California,
  Berkeley
Pelto, Chester R. 1971. 'The statistical structure of bidding for oil and mineral
  rights.' *Journal of the American Statistical Association* 66: 456-60
Porter, Robert H. 1983. 'Optimal cartel trigger price strategies.' *Journal of
  Economic Theory* 29: 313-38
Provincial Auditor of Ontario. 1983. *Annual Report*. Toronto
Quirk, James, and Katsuaki Terasawa. 1984. 'The winner's curse and cost
  estimation bias in pioneer projects.' Working Paper No. 512, California
  Institute of Technology
Radner, Roy. 1981. 'Monitoring cooperative agreements in a repeated principal-
  agent relationship.' *Econometrica* 49: 1127-48
Ramsey, James B. 1983. 'Empirical analysis on lease bidding using historical
  data.' In R. Engelbrecht-Wiggans, M. Shubik, and R.M. Stark, eds.,
  Auctions, Bidding, and Contracting. New York: New York University Press
Rao, C. Radhakrishna. 1973. *Linear Statistical Inference and Its Applications*.
  New York: John Wiley & Sons

Reece, Douglas K. 1978. 'Competitive bidding for offshore petroleum leases.
'*Bell Journal of Economics* 9: 369-84

Reichelstein, Stefan, and Kent Osband. 1984. 'Incentives in government
contracts.' *Journal of Public Economics* 24: 257-70

Reinganum, Jennifer F., and Louis Wilde. 1984. 'Income tax compliance in a
principal-agent framework.' Mimeo. California Institute of Technology

Reuber, Grant L. 1980. 'Coping with rising health costs.' Chapter 8 of *Canada's
Political Economy*. Toronto: McGraw-Hill Ryerson

Riemer, W.H. 1968. *Handbook of Government Contract Administration*.
Englewood Cliffs, NJ: Prentice-Hall

Riley, John G., and William F. Samuelson. 1981. 'Optimal auctions.' *American
Economic Review* 71: 381-92

Robson, A.J., and J. McMillan. 1984. 'Dynamic duopoly under demand
uncertainty.' *Canadian Journal of Economics* 17: 695-9

Rogerson, William P. 1983. 'The first-order approach to the principal-agent
problem.' Mimeo. Stanford University

Rubenstein, Ariel. 1979. 'An optimal conviction policy for offences that may
have been committed by accident.' In S.J.Brams, A. Schotter, and
G. Schwödiaur, eds., *Applied Game Theory*. Würzburg: Physica-Verlag

Samuelson, William F. 1983. 'Competitive bidding for incentive contracts.' In
R. Engelbrecht-Wiggans, M. Shubik, and R.M. Stark, eds., *Auctions,
Bidding, and Contracting: Uses and Theory*. New York: New York
University Press

- 1984. 'Bidding for contracts.' Discussion Paper No. 32/84, School of
Management, Boston University

- 1985. 'Competitive bidding with entry costs.' *Economics Letters* 17: 53-7

Savas, E.S. 1982. *Privatizing the Public Sector*. Chatham, NJ: Chatham House

Scherer, Frederic M. 1964a. 'The theory of contractual incentives for cost
reduction.' *Quarterly Journal of Economics* 78: 257-80

- 1964b. *The Weapons Acquisition Process: Economic Incentives*. Cambridge:
Graduate School of Business Administration, Harvard University

- 1970. *Industrial Market Structure and Economic Performance*. Chicago:
Rand McNally

Shavell, Steven. 1979. 'Risk sharing and incentives in the principal and agent
relationship.' *Bell Journal of Economics* 10: 55-73

- 1984. 'The design of contracts and remedies for breach.' *Quarterly Journal
of Economics* 99: 121-48

Sinn, Hans-Werner. 1983. *Economic Decisions under Uncertainty*. Amsterdam:
North-Holland

Smith, Adam. 1976. *An Enquiry into the Nature and Causes of the Wealth of
Nations*. Edited by E. Cannan. Chicago: University of Chicago Press

Starrett, David. 1983. 'On the marginal cost of government spending.' Technical
Report No. 426, Institute for Mathematical Studies in the Social Sciences,
Stanford University

Steinberg, Bruce. 1984. 'The military boost to industry.' *Fortune*, April: 30, 42-8

Stigler, George J. 1964. 'A theory of oligopoly.' *Journal of Political Economy* 72: 44-61

- 1975. *The Citizen and the State*. Chicago: University of Chicago Press

Stuart, Charles. 1984. 'Welfare costs per dollar of additional tax revenue in the United States.' *American Economic Review* 74: 352-62

Supapol, A.B., and D.G. McFetridge. 1982. 'An analysis of the federal make-or-buy policy.' Discussion Paper No. 217, Economic Council of Canada

Terasawa, Katsuaki, James Quirk, and Keith Womar. 1984. 'Turbulence, cost escalation, and capital intensity bias in defense contracting.' Working Paper No. 508, California Institute of Technology

Theil, Henri. 1981. 'The maximum entropy principle, chapter 1.' Mimeo. University of Florida

Tirole, Jean. 1984. 'Procurement, cost overruns and severance: a study in commitment and renegotiation.' Mimeo. CERAS, Ecole Nationale des Ponts et Chausées

Townsend, Robert M. 1979. 'Optimal contracts and competitive markets with costly state verification.' *Journal of Economic Theory* 21: 265-93

Treasury Board of Canada. 1980. *Administrative Policy Manual*. Ottawa

Trebilcock, Michael J., John Whalley, Carol Rogerson, and Jan Ness. 1983. 'Provincially induced barriers to trade in Canada: a survey.' In M.J. Trebilcock et al., eds., *Federalism and the Canadian Economic Union*. Toronto: Ontario Economic Council

United States. 1984. *President's Private Sector Survey on Cost Control: Report to the President*. Vols. 1 and 2. Washington, DC: US Government Printing Office

Viner, Jacob. 1943. *Trade Relations between Free-Market and Controlled Economies*. Geneva: League of Nations

Weitzman, Martin L. 1980. 'Efficient incentive contracts.' *Quarterly Journal of Economics* 44: 719-30

Westing, H.H., I.V. Fine, and G.J. Zenz. 1976. *Purchasing Management*. New York: John Wiley & Sons

Yuspeh, Larry. 1976. 'A case for increasing the use of competitive procurement in the Department of Defense.' In Y. Amihud, ed., *Bidding and Auctioning for Procurement and Allocation*. New York: New York University Press

Indexes

NAME INDEX

www.ingramcontent.com/pod-product-compliance
Lightning Source LLC
Chambersburg PA
CBHW030516210326
41597CB00013B/931